The Legal World
of the School Principal

The Legal World
of the School Principal

What Leaders Need to Know about School Law

M. Scott Norton

ROWMAN & LITTLEFIELD
Lanham • Boulder • New York • London

Published by Rowman & Littlefield
A wholly owned subsidiary of The Rowman & Littlefield Publishing Group, Inc.
4501 Forbes Boulevard, Suite 200, Lanham, Maryland 20706
www.rowman.com

Unit A, Whitacre Mews, 26-34 Stannary Street, London SE11 4AB

British Library Cataloguing in Publication Information Available

Library of Congress Cataloging-in-Publication Data

Names: Norton, M. Scott, author.
Title: The legal world of the school principal : what leaders need to know about school law / M. Scott Norton.
Description: Lanham, Maryland : Rowman & Littlefield Education, 2016. | Includes bibliographical references.
Identifiers: LCCN 2016011789 (print) | LCCN 2016012219 (ebook) | ISBN 9781475823479 (cloth : alk. paper) | ISBN 9781475823486 (pbk. : alk. paper) | ISBN 9781475823493 (electronic)
Subjects: LCSH: School principals--Legal status, laws, etc.--United States. | Educational law and legislation--United States.
Classification: LCC KF4133 .N67 2016 (print) | LCC KF4133 (ebook) | DDC 344.73/07--dc23
LC record available at http://lccn.loc.gov/2016011789

♾ ™ The paper used in this publication meets the minimum requirements of American National Standard for Information Sciences Permanence of Paper for Printed Library Materials, ANSI/NISO Z39.48-1992.

Printed in the United States of America

Contents

Preface

The primary focus of this book is to emphasize what school assistant principals, principals, and other administrative leaders must know regarding school law and to underscore the necessity for them to be fully knowledgeable of their legal responsibilities and liabilities when working directly with teacher personnel, students, and parents in exercising their daily responsibilities. As noted by Peterson, Rossmiller, and Volz more than forty years ago:

> Legal enactments and interpretations are having a far-reaching influence on the lives of all who are associated with the schools—children, parents, teachers, supervisors, administrators, and members of boards of education. . . . An understanding of these legislative enactments and judicial interpretations within the framework of legal principles is basic to sound operational practice and to effective decision making in classrooms, administrative circles, board meetings and communities as well as in intermediate districts and at state and federal levels. (p. ix)

Federal laws, state statutes, and legal interpretations by the courts at various levels establish school law. Since the U.S. Constitution makes no reference to education, it always has been assumed that education is the responsibility of the several states. Unless specifically legislated by the federal government or as the result of case law, a particular school law on the same subject commonly differs in some ways from state to state. Thus, it is quite impossible to set forth a common law on topics such as employee substance abuse, teacher evaluation, insubordination, and others that can be applied to all fifty states.

Federal laws, state statutes, and court decisions have significant impacts on school law. In addition, school boards are responsible for adopting school policies that set forth the aims/purposes of a school district, and local school superintendents and the professional staff develop accompanying administrative regulations. Specific school rules relating to student behavior, absenteeism, homework, bullying, and other activities tie closely to the complex topic of school law. Teacher personnel administration requires a substantial knowledge of school law as well.

Although the book has specific implications for the work of the school assistant principal and principal, other school leaders will find the content of special value to them as well. Research results have indicated that school principals are facing serious legal issues and problems in their leadership role. In addition, a limited percentage of school principals state that they were not well prepared to deal with the various legal matters facing them in the role.

SPECIAL FEATURES OF THE BOOK

The book will be of special help to aspiring school assistant principals, principals, teachers, parents, school board members, and others that are involved in educational activities in schools for understanding and meeting the legal requirements related to school operation by:

- Clarifying the purposes, characteristics, and differences between the terms *school policies*, *administrative regulations*, and *school rules*—terms that are commonly misused by educators themselves.
- Presenting the different ways that school policies and administrative regulations can be appropriately codified for ease of referencing and logical organization.
- Discussing many of the landmark legal cases that have influenced educational practices in America's schools.
- Using reader engagement in the chapters' information through the use of pre-quizzes, snapshots, and lightbulb experiences.
- Discussing specifically the school leader's responsibilities relative to such matters as student safety and welfare, student hearings, corporal punishment, locker searches, and other matters relating to student rights and restrictions.
- Presenting the legal responsibilities of school leaders relative to faculty and staff personnel administration.
- Providing opportunities for the reader to extend his/her learning by including discussion questions, case studies, and a list of reading references at the end of each chapter.
- Using a reader-friendly style that commonly brings the reader into the context of situations being discussed.

- Answering many questions of paramount importance that will increase the confidence of school leaders dealing with legal matters encountered daily in school administration.
- Including the landmark cases that have influenced the administration activities of school leaders nationally and also numerous court cases that have underscored the legal rights of students, administrators, teachers, and parents as related to education in America.
- Presenting pre-quizzes in each chapter that serve as a set for the chapter's discussions and emphasizing the importance of various legal rulings that are influencing the work of school leaders.

ORGANIZATION OF THE BOOK

The book is presented in four chapters that serve to define, explain, and emphasize the knowledge needed by school leaders relative to working in their legal world. Chapter 1 presents the foundation for legal authority in America and discusses major landmark cases that have affected legal governance since the adoption of the U.S. Constitution. Chapter 2 centers on the legal rights and liabilities of school principals. Chapter 3 focuses on the legal rights and liabilities of teacher personnel, and chapter 4 centers on the legal rights and liabilities of students.

Each chapter is appropriately summarized by setting forth the major concepts and knowledge presented. A set of discussion questions for the readers' consideration is included at the close of each chapter. In addition, case studies that place the reader in a specific position for dealing with a legal question/situation also are set forth at the end of each chapter.

The appendix includes a glossary of legal terms, selected court cases for further consideration by the reader, and significant historical events in education that have influenced programs and procedures.

Chapter One

How the Legal Responsibilities of School Leaders Are Determined and Implemented

Primary chapter goal: To present the primary governmental sources that establish and administer the laws, statutes, policies, and regulations that impact on the governance of education in America and underscore the vital importance of the legal responsibilities and liabilities of school leaders.

THE U.S. CONSTITUTION AS THE SUPREME LAW OF THE LAND

Within the provisions of the U.S. Constitution and through the legal enactments of the federal government, state legislatures, and local government bodies, the programs of education in America are defined. The Constitution makes no reference to education; historically, it has been assumed that education is the responsibility of the fifty separate states. As stated by the Tenth Amendment to the Constitution: "The powers not delegated to the United States by the Constitution, nor prohibited by it by the States, are reserved to the States respectively, or to the people." This statement permits state legislatures to approve any educational legislation not prohibited by other legal action.

The Preamble of the U.S. Constitution sets forth the paramount importance of the document.

> We the people of the United States, in order to form a more perfect union, establish justice, ensure domestic tranquility, provide for the common defense, promote the general welfare, and secure the blessings of liberty do establish and ordain this Constitution for the United States of America.

1

Article I of the U.S. Constitution states that all *legislative powers* herein granted shall be vested in a Congress of the United States that shall consist of a Senate and House of Representatives. Article III, Section 1 states: "The judicial power of the United States, shall be vested in one Supreme Court, and in such inferior Courts as the Congress from time to time ordain and establish." Thus, the final authority in the land is the United States Supreme Court. Rulings from the United States Court of Appeals are second highest for judicial decisions. Rulings from a United States Circuit Court of Appeals are binding over the Courts in the states of that Circuit.

The U.S. Supreme Court ultimately determines the constitutionality of acts passed by the U.S. Congress. The constitutionality of executive orders set forth by a president of the United States is subject to the rulings of the Supreme Court. Although Congress or a state Supreme Court might disagree with the decision of the U.S. Supreme Court, the U.S. Supreme Court ruling stands. The president of the United States nominates members of the U.S. Supreme Court, but they must receive approval by the U.S. Senate. As stated in the Constitution, the president "shall nominate and by the advice and consent of the Senate shall appoint Supreme Court and all other officers of the United States, whose appointments are not herein otherwise provided for, and which shall be established by law."

A simple majority vote is needed by the Senate to approve a nominee's appointment to the Supreme Court. In addition, Supreme Court appointees "shall hold their offices during good behavior," which has been interpreted to mean the rest of their lives.

THE UNITED STATES AND THE RIGHTS OF ITS PEOPLE

A small survey of citizens that focused on the First Amendment revealed that only a small number of citizens knew what the First Amendment to the Constitution was about, and they could not describe what rights the amendment actually included. For this reason and because the first ten amendments consist of the Bill of Rights for all citizens of the United States, the first fifteen amendments are succinctly presented in the following sections. Later in the chapter, these amendments are presented in more detail.

First Amendment—Congress shall make no law respecting an establishment of religion, or prohibiting the exercise thereof, or abridging the freedom of speech, or of the press; or of the right of the people peaceably to assemble, and to petition the government for a redress of grievances.

Second Amendment—A well-regulated Militia, being necessary to the security of a free state, the right of the people to keep and bear arms, shall not be infringed.

Third Amendment—No soldier shall, in time of peace, be quartered in any house without the owner's consent, forbidding the practice in peacetime.

Fourth Amendment—The right of the people to be secure in their persons, houses, papers, and effects, against unreasonable searches and seizures, shall not be violated and no warrants shall issue, but upon probable cause, supported by Oath or affirmation.

Fifth Amendment—No person shall be held to answer for capital, or otherwise infamous crime, unless on a presentment or indictment of a grand jury, except in cases arising in the land or naval forces, or in the militia, when in actual service in time of war or public danger (cannot witness against one's self).

Sixth Amendment—In criminal prosecutions, the accused shall enjoy the right to speedy and public trial, by an impartial jury of the State and district wherein the crime shall have been committed.

Seventh Amendment—In suits at common law, where the value in controversy shall exceed twenty dollars, the right of trial by jury shall be preserved and no fact tried by a jury, shall otherwise be reexamined in any Court of the United States, than according to the rules of common law.

Eighth Amendment—Excessive bail shall not be required, nor excessive fines imposed, nor cruel and unusual punishment inflicted.

Ninth Amendment—The enumeration in the Constitution, of certain rights, shall not be construed to deny or disparage others retained by the people (people do have other rights).

Tenth Amendment—The amendment further defined the balance of power between the federal government and states. Powers not granted to the United States were reserved to the states or to the people.

Eleventh Amendment—The judicial power of the United States shall not be construed to extend to any suit in law or equity, commanded or prosecuted against one of the United States by citizens of another state, or by citizens or subjects of a foreign state (no one can sue a state in federal court without the consent of the state).

Twelfth Amendment—Provided for the election of the president and vice president by electoral college.

Thirteenth Amendment—Abolished slavery in the United States.

Fourteenth Amendment—Granted citizenship to all persons born or naturalized in the United States.

Fifteenth Amendment—Protects the rights of Americans to elect their leaders.

FEDERAL COURT SYSTEM

Figure 1.1 illustrates the organization of the federal court system and the common organization of court authority that begins with the U.S. Supreme Court.

FEDERAL COURT SYSTEM

UNITED STATES SUPREME COURT

WASHINGTON, D.C.

APPEALS FROM	UNITED STATES COURT OF
STATE COURTS	CUSTOMS AND PATENT APPEALS

UNITED STATES COURT OF APPEALS

CUSTOM COURT	
UNITED STATES	DISTRICTS
COURT OF CLAIMS	UNITED STATES DISTRICT COURTS
	UNITED STATES TERRITORIAL COURTS
TAX COURT	U.S. COURT OF MILITARY APPEALS
ADMINISTRATIVE	U.S. Military COURT-MARTIALS
AGENCIES	

Figure 1.1.   Federal Court System

LISTING OF LANDMARK COURT CASES

Over the years, there have been a number of landmark court cases that have established important legal standards or practices nationally. Landmark cases have significant impact on judicial proceedings by prompting the creation of new laws and legal precedents. We examined several listings of landmark cases and are of the opinion that the following court cases are among the leading ones that can be viewed as landmark cases. Our purpose is to identify these cases to illustrate just how some of them are frequently revealed nationally in the rulings of other court cases and the passing of state statutes. Several other landmark cases are discussed later in the book.

Marbury v. Madison, 5. U.S. 137 (1803)—This court case helped define the boundary between the constitutionally separate branches of the American form of government. In effect, the U.S. Supreme Court was judged to act as an arbitrator between the states and between the federal government and a state.

Brown v. Board of Education, 347 U.S. 483 (1954)—Held that the racial segregation of children in public schools violated the Equal Protection Clause of the Fourteenth Amendment.

New York Times v. Sullivan, 376 U.S. 254 (1964)—Established the actual malice standard that has to be met before press reports can be considered to be defamation and libel; thus it allowed free reporting of the civil rights campaigns.

Griswold v. Connecticut, 381 U.S. 479, 85 S. Ct. 1678, 14 L. Ed. (1965)—Ruled that the Constitution protected a right to privacy. The right to privacy is seen as a right to protection from government intrusion.

Miranda v. Arizona, 384 U.S. 436 (1966)—Held that statements made in response to interrogation by a defendant in police custody will be admissible at trial only if the prosecution can show that the defendant was informed of the right to consult an attorney before and during questioning and the right against self-incrimination before police questioning, and the defendant not only understood these rights but also voluntarily waived them.

TIME OUT FOR A PRE-QUIZ ON SCHOOL LAW

The Pre-Quiz: Circle true or false to each of the following statements relating to the law as it influences federal, state, and local educational policies and procedures. Don't just guess an answer; rather, skip that question and move on to the next one.

True or False

1. The U.S. Constitution makes no mention of education and has delegated those powers not set forth in the Constitution to the many states. Therefore, the federal government has refrained from establishing policies and/or setting forth mandates for local school operations. ___T or ___F
2. The federal government substantially supports public education as revealed in the fact that it presently provides approximately 52 percent of the total annual funding for public school education programs. ___T or ___F
3. The U.S. Supreme Court has made a special effort to refrain from accepting legal cases relating to education since education historically is viewed as a responsibility of the many states. ___T or ___F
4. The original Department of Education (federal) was created in 1867. However, in 1980 that department was abolished and nothing has been done since to give education a federal office for educational purposes. ___T or ___F

5. In 2009, the U.S. Supreme Court ruled President Obama's Race to the Top program unconstitutional since its focus on a Common Core of Educational Standards violated the rights of the states. ___T or ___F

6. The U.S. Supreme Court has generally deferred to state and local governments the rights to deal with student discipline and to intervene in cases of mistreatment. ___T or ___F

7. Statutory law is defined as the body of law derived from constitutions or judicial decisions. ___T or ___F

8. The U.S. Constitution provides that all legislative powers of the federal government be vested in a Congress consisting of a Senate and House of Representatives. ___T or ___F

9. The body of law that makes up the collection of reported cases that include all or part of the body of law within a jurisdiction is known as the "book of statutes." ___T or ___F

10. A law is a rule recognized by the nation or state as binding on its members. ___T or ___F

11. A bylaw is a procedure by which a legal body and/or member organization governs itself. ___T or ___F

12. A school board policy is a precise statement that answers the question of *how* a policy is to be applied or implemented. ___ T or ___F

13. An administrative regulation is equivalent to legislation and is a broad statement that allows for freedom of interpretation and execution. ___T or ___F

14. A school district policy can either be authorized by the school board or by a committee appointed by the school board consisting of the school superintendent, a school principal, a teacher within the district, a school parent, and a current student in grades ten through twelve. ___T or ___F

15. All state school superintendents (not local school district superintendents) are appointed by the governor of the state in which they serve. ___T or ___F

Answers to the Pre-Quiz

Answer 1 is False; 2 is False; 3 is False; 4 is False; 5 is False; 6 is True; 7 is False; 8 is True; 9 is False; 10 is True; 11 is True; 12 is False; 13 is False; 14 is False; and 15 is False.

Your Scoring Status

15–13 correct: You are a member of your state's Supreme Court.

12–10 correct: You can serve as legal advisor for a school district.

9–7 correct: You passed the Bar.

6–4 correct: Retake the quiz after studying chapter 1.

3–1 correct: Study chapter 1 carefully.

A Brief Response to Each Pre-Quiz Question

1. Question 1, the federal government has refrained from establishing policies and/or setting mandates for public school operations, is false. In fact, just the opposite is true. This chapter and others that follow will show the federal government and federal court's strong involvement in educational concerns relative to the welfare of the nation. Historically, there always has been a "yes" and "no" position on the federal government's involvement in education. The positive side argues that federal involvement is the one entity that can assure equal access and opportunity for the education of all children and youth. In addition, the federal government's financial support of education has been instrumental in promoting specific programs that center on the nation's special needs. On the other hand, the negative side submits that federal involvement in education inhibits the power of the states to do what is best for its citizens. While the federal government is giving a low level of financial support for public schools, it is demanding high levels of control. Many of the federal government's mandates are established without the needed funds to carry them out effectively. Unfunded mandates continue to be one of education's difficult problems.
2. Question 2, the federal government provides 52 percent of the total funding for public schools annually, is false. In reality, the federal government's financial support for public education annually is approximately 11 percent. It is true that the support figure for the federal government's funding is a complex matter and quite difficult to calculate. Nevertheless, both the local school district and the state in which the school resides provide a much greater portion of the funding for public school operations.
3. Question 3, the federal government has resisted accepting legal cases relating to the operation of public schools, is false. As further reading in this and other chapters of the book will reveal, the federal government and U.S. Supreme Court have been essentially involved in legal rulings relative to most all phases of school operations.
4. Question 4, in 1980, the U.S. Department of Education was abolished and nothing has been done since to give education a federal office, is false. In 1980, the Department of Education was given cabinet status by Congress. Although attempts to disestablish the cabinet position have been talked about from time to time, the department remains in operation after some thirty-six years and continues to serve the nation's school districts in America.
5. Question 5, President Obama's Race to the Top educational program was ruled unconstitutional, is false. Race to the Top is a multi-billion-

dollar federal program implemented for the purpose of fostering creative reforms in education in the United States. It is a competitive program that gives points for funding related to great teachers and leaders, state success factors, standards and assessments, significant reform improvements, improving lowest-performing schools, and installing a data system for improving and supporting instruction. Early complaints about the program centered on the facts that only a few school districts actually were receiving monies from the program, and the funding decisions, reportedly, tended to center on the politics of selecting "winning school districts."

6. Question 6, the federal government has generally deferred to state and local governments the rights to deal with student discipline and to intervene in cases of mistreatment, is true. It is commonly assumed that the position of a teacher has the authority to establish rules that serve to control student conduct. In the same way, the courts have supported the authority for school administrators to establish and enforce rules of conduct that maintain the order necessary for conducting an effective learning atmosphere in the school.

   The "principle" of in loco parentis whereby the teacher assumes the role and authority of a parent is somewhat troublesome. Reportedly, some states are finding the in loco parentis concept of special benefit when discussing the rights of teachers in their disciplinary roles. However, the concept most commonly is restricted to student control and not to all educational matters. For example, "In private matters unrelated to education, the teacher stands outside the concept of in loco parentis" (Peterson et al., 1978, p. 347).

7. Question 7, statutory law is defined as the body of law derived from constitutions or judicial decisions, is false. Statutory laws are based on rulings established by legislative bodies such as state legislatures. When a state legislature passes a bill, it becomes a law. The provisions of the law are termed *statutes.*

8. Question 8, the U.S. Constitution provides that all legislative powers of the federal government be vested in a Congress consisting of a Senate and a House of Representatives, is true (Article I, Section 1 of the U.S. Constitution).

9. Question 9, the body of law that makes up the collection of reported cases that include all or part of the body of law written in a jurisdiction is known as the book of statutes, is false. Rather, that body of law is *case law*.

10. Question 10, a law is a rule recognized by the state or nation as binding on its members, is true. A law is derived by an action of one of the branches of government. However, since there exists several different branches of government, a law enacted by one branch of

government is not necessarily binding on other branches of government. In all cases, however, the court of higher jurisdiction is favored and supersedes any law determined by a lesser government. Within a state, the state's Supreme Court is the final authority. Nationally, the U.S. Supreme Court is the final law of the land.

11. Question 11, a bylaw is a procedure by which a legal body and/or member organization governs itself, is true. For example, the bylaws of a school board of education would center on the way it will operate, how board officers will be elected and time of service, board meeting dates and time, subcommittee arrangements, executive meetings, policy development, and other organizational arrangements. A school board's authority commonly is viewed as formal authority and functional authority. *Formal authority* is based on the legislative powers given to the school board by the state's constitution or by legislative statute. *Functional authority* is viewed as the level of competence and human characteristics of the persons that occupy positions on the school board.

12. Question 12, a school board policy is a precise statement that answers the question of how a policy is to be applied or implemented, is false. On the contrary, a school policy answers the question of what it is that the school is to do or strive toward. Policies are considered as legislative documents that deal with highly important matters that the school district faces; policies represent the purposes and objectives of the school board. School board policy development is discussed at length later in the chapter.

13. Question 13, an administrative regulation is equivalent to legislation and is a broad statement that allows for freedom of interpretation and execution, is false. An effective administrative regulation is specific in setting forth how it is to be administered in practice. A regulation is executive in nature in that it commonly specifies steps for its implementation and establishes the responsible persons for its implementation and accountability for desired results.

14. Question 14, a school policy can be adopted by the school or by a committee consisting of the school superintendent and other members of the school community, is false. Only the school board can adopt school policies, although in more recent history, school policies are based on federal and state legislative mandates and state court rulings. This topic is discussed in more detail later in the chapter.

15. Question 15, all state school superintendents (not school district superintendents) are appointed by the governors of each of the fifty states, is false. At the time of this writing, the number of states that appointed the superintendent of public instruction was approximately the same as the ones that elected the person to the position. So, is the

superintendent of public instruction subject to the calling of the state's electorate, or is he or she responsible to the governor of the state? The answer depends solely on state statutes. This question was being "argued" in the state of Arizona at the time of this writing.

AMENDMENTS I, IV, VII, X, XIV, AND TITLE VII OF THE CIVIL RIGHTS ACT OF THE U.S. CONSTITUTION

Amendments I, IV, VII, X, XIV, and Title VII of the Civil Rights Act of 1964 historically have had major impacts on practices in education. Amendment I centers on the freedom of religion, press, and expression. Amendment I and other constitutional amendments are as follows:

Amendment I—Freedom of Religion, Press, and Expression. Congress shall make no law respecting an establishment of religion, or prohibiting the free exercise thereof; or abridging the freedom of speech, or of the press, or the right of the people peaceably to assemble, and to petition the government, for a redress of grievances. Amendment I has served foundationally in court decisions at the state and national levels.

Amendment IV—Search and Seizure. The right of the people to be secure in their persons, houses, papers, and effects, against unreasonable searches and seizures, shall not be violated, and no Warrants shall issue, but upon probable cause, supported by Oath or affirmation, and particularly describing the place to be searched, and the persons or things to be seized. Privacy has been a common concern of court rulings relative to student locker searches and searches of the person.

Amendment X—Delegation of Powers to the States (previously mentioned in the chapter).

Amendment XIV, Section 1—Citizenship and the Rights of Citizens. All persons born or naturalized in the United States, and subject to jurisdiction thereof, as citizens of the United States and the state wherein they reside. No state shall make or enforce any laws that shall abridge the privileges or immunities of citizens of the United States; nor shall any state deprive any person of life, liberty, or property without due process of law; nor deny to any person within its jurisdiction the equal protection of the law. Citizen rights continue to be a major issue in the United States. Immigration and citizenship is among the major issues facing the nation presently.

Title VII, Section 703, of the Civil Rights Act of 1964. Prohibits discrimination based on race, color, religion, or sex. The title states that it shall be unlawful to discriminate against any individual with respect to his compensation, terms, conditions, or privileges of employment because of such individual's race, color, religion, sex, or national origin. In addition, rights set forth by Title VII have been extended to employment opportunities for individuals with disabilities, age discrimination, and other rights of students and school employees.

THE FEDERAL GOVERNMENT AND INFLUENCE ON EDUCATION

Historically, education has been viewed as a national concern, a state responsibility, and a local function. In view of the provisions of the Tenth Amendment and its delegated authority to the states, it would seem that the federal government has little to do with education. Certainly, the federal government's involvement in education has been far and above a concern. The record shows that the federal government has had and continues to have a strong involvement in educational matters. Through enactments related to the U.S. Constitution and Supreme Court decisions, the federal government has had significant influences on educational practices in such areas as civil rights, church and state rulings, vocational education measures, student physical fitness measures, special education provisions, and others.

Approximately fifty years ago, Tiedt (1966) authored an excellent account of the federal government's role in education. He summarized the chronological summary of federal legislation from 1777 to the date of his published book, 1966. For the 239 years, Tiedt listed fifty-six specific pieces of federal legislation that centered on federal aid to education. The listing began with the 1777 initiation of the direct administration of education programs—the instruction of military personnel, including schooling in mathematics, to the introduction of the principle of federal-state matching of funds for education in 1874, to the National Defense Education Act of 1968, to the Higher Education Act for aid to colleges, students, and teachers in 1965.

The federal controls on educational programs and practices are evident even though its financial support for education is lowest among the three levels of local, state, and federal government. Fifty-six years ago, in 1959, states were receiving approximately 1 percent of their educational support from the federal government (Norton, 1959, p. 84). Overall, it is estimated that the federal government presently provides approximately 10 percent of the annual funds received for education. Individual states now provide the greatest financial support for education, with local school support being second highest in school funding.

It is clear that states must follow the decisions of the Supreme Court and cannot refuse to obey them. This fact applies to all educational practices and was substantiated by the Supreme Court's decision in the case of *Cooper v. Aaron* (1958), whereby the court recognized the state's responsibility for education but stated that the state's activity must be consistently exercised within federal constitutionality.

Figure 1.2 shows various ways in which the federal government has demonstrated its concern for public education in America. The entries represent selected program interventions that will be discussed in various chapters throughout this book.

Land Ordinances and Grants

Vocational Education

Military Impact Aid Laws

Agricultural, Industrial, Home Ec Training

Title I Funding

No Child Left Behind Legislation

Race to the Top Legislation

Federal Government & K-12 Education

NDEA Act

Civil Rights Act

Head Start

Special Education Legislation

Early Childhood Legislation

Child Care Development Fund

School Lunch Programs

Rehabilitation Act

ESEA Act, Title I

IDEA-Individuals w/ Disabilities

Title IX-Prohibit Discrimination

Nation at Risk

Figure 1.2.   Examples of Educational Program Activities by the Federal Government

THE STATES AND STATUTORY LAW

The laws that have been discussed previously evolve from the constitution or by rulings of the various courts. Laws derived from legal bodies such as state legislatures are termed *statutes.* All states have a state legislature and commonly are bicameral in organization with an upper body of the senate and a lower body of representatives. Nebraska, for example, has a unicameral legislature to which all elected members belong. The term *cameral* comes from the Latin word *camera*, meaning "chamber." Thus a unicameral legislature has one chamber or legislative house. A bicameral legislature has two houses, commonly the House of Representatives and the Senate.

BRIEFING A LAW CASE

One might have the occasion to brief law cases that support the school's opinion of a current lawsuit. In that case, a law briefing commonly includes the following information.

1. Title: The specific title for the law case being briefed is set forth with the proper citation.
2. Facts: The facts of the case are stated briefly. The circumstances that put the case in the courts are noted. This statement represents the background events surrounding the case.
3. Issues: The issues of the case are stated. The issues represent what had to be decided/settled by the court.
4. Decision: What was the court's ruling? What was the reason for making the ruling? In cases of a state's Supreme Court decision, the opinion of the majority court members is stated. This is especially true when there is a divided court opinion (e.g., 5 to 4 vote).
5. Significance: What implication does the ruling(s) in the case have for school personnel?

THE STATE COURT SYSTEM

Each state has a court system that is independent of federal courts. State court systems have trial courts at the bottom and appellate courts at the top. Reportedly, over 95 percent of the nation's legal cases are decided in state courts or in local courts that are agents of the state. State court systems do differ organizationally, but they have common levels of court authority. Figure 1.3 illustrates a common court system.

STATE SUPREME COURT

STATE COURT OF APPEALS

Division 1-Departments

Division 2—Courts, Judges

SUPERIOR COURTS

JUVENILE COURTS   PROBATE COURTS   JUSTICE OF THE PEACE COURTS

MUNICIPAL COURTS—Civil and Criminal Matters

SMALL CLAIMS COURTS   TRAFFIC COURTS   CITY COURTS

Figure 1.3.   State Court System

STATE BOARDS OF EDUCATION

State departments of education and state boards of education are outcomes of actions by the state government. State boards of education commonly have a state superintendent that is either elected by ballot or appointed by the state Board of Education. Interestingly enough, states that elect the state superintendent commonly are faced with a public that is of the opinion that the superintendent should be appointed. On the other hand, those states that appoint the superintendent tend to argue that he or she should be elected. We know of no evidence that one way is better or worse than the other.

THE BASIS FOR STATES' RESPONSIBILITY FOR EDUCATION

Amendment X of the U.S. Constitution reserves powers to states for matters not specifically delegated to the federal government or prohibited to the states or to the people. Since the specific educational authority of the states is not established within the constitution, it is able to establish statutes for controlling education just as long as superior laws do not forbid them. One such superior law would be the constitution of the state. The state's constitution often serves as the restraint for enacting a certain educational statute. At the same time, a state's Supreme Court would constitute the final authority within the state for approving or prohibiting the enactment of an educational statute.

As a school professional, it is important that you understand that your local school board is an extension of the state legislature. That is, the board's authority is vested in the fact that the state legislature has delegated certain responsibilities to local school districts. Even though the legislature has done so, it does not mean that the legislature has delegated its legislative powers to the local school district. What the state legislature has done is to delegate certain administrative authority to the local school board. As pointed out by

Peterson and others (1978), "Courts hold that it is the function of the state to provide and promote an efficient educational program and that school laws are to be liberally construed to effect a beneficial purpose" (p. 9).

Peterson and others (1978) underscore the control of local school boards as delegated by the state board of education. It cannot be assumed that the state has relinquished its control over education. Court rulings have made it clear that when the state relinquishes its authority regarding the local control of the school district, it absolutely does not relinquish its control over education when it does so. In fact, early courts have ruled that the state legislature can change the controlling agencies as it sees fit at any time (*Hasbrouck v. School Committee*, 128, ATl. 449 [R.I. 1925]).

OTHER RESPONSIBILITIES/OPERATIONS OF STATE BOARDS OF EDUCATION

Although the legal responsibilities of state boards of education do differ, the state board commonly is involved in curriculum issues, student testing programs, teacher performance evaluation requirements, tenure provisions, teacher/administrator licensing, student achievement standards, school accreditation, student discipline, compulsory school attendance, special education programs, vocational education, charter schools, and other educational activities and programs.

The authority of state school boards is provided commonly either by the state's constitution or by statute. At the time of this writing, a major controversy in Arizona was present over the question as to whether the state school board was under the supervision/control of the governor or of the elected state superintendent of public instruction. Staff personnel that were housed within the offices of the state school superintendent were ordered by the newly elected governor to move from the superintendent's offices to other offices within the governor's jurisdiction. A lawsuit on this matter is pending at the time of this writing.

THE COUNTY SUPERINTENDENT'S OFFICE

The early rapid population growth and increases in urban living in the United States made it impossible for states to supervise effectively school operations. The immediate answer was the development of the county superintendent's office that served to provide better state control over school districts in the state. Delaware is given credit for having the first county superintendency as early as 1827. Keep in mind that schoolteachers were "ill prepared" for the job of teaching at that time in history, and many elementary school teachers began teaching school immediately after graduating from high school.

There were no teacher training programs operating in the early 1800s, and teacher training was a desperate need. Reports indicate that by 1879, approximately 63 percent of the thirty-eight states had county superintendents. Henry Barnard, member of the Connecticut legislature and later the first U.S. Commissioner of Education, reportedly put up his own funds to establish the first teacher institute for the purpose of learning teaching principles and the use of materials. Teachers welcomed the teacher institutes, which eventually graduated into the first two-year normal schools that centered on teacher preparation.

Today, the responsibilities of county superintendents and county school boards vary widely and commonly are determined by whatever is set forth by the state's legislative bodies. Legal descriptions of the office of county superintendent commonly are stated simply as the county superintendent being a constitution officer. Attempts to provide a more specific meaning of this description fall short of the mark. Peterson and others (1978) state: "In states with county unit districts the county superintendent has broad instructional responsibilities, akin to the broad responsibilities of local superintendents of schools" (p. 21). Such responsibilities were not elaborated.

THE GOVERNANCE OF THE LOCAL SCHOOL BOARD

The authority given a school board is received from the state's constitution or from statutes enacted by the state's legislature. As an extension of the state legislature, a school board is given the authority to approve policies that set forth the goals/purposes of the school district. School boards as a whole can act to do those things necessary to assure the proper maintenance and effectiveness of the school district's educational program. However, individual members of a school have no authority/power to act officially; only the board acting as a legal whole can adopt policies or take other actions that are given to them by the state's constitution or by state statutes.

It is true that many acts of school boards have been established without the evidence of reference in the state's constitution and/or by legislative action. For example, school lunch programs and student health services have been identified as within the authority of the school board mainly after the fact. That is, the practice has become widespread within schools on the basis that a school board considered them as being within their authority to implement. However, state legislatures and the courts have been quick to deny and/or limit the board's authority when it believes that such authority has been overextended.

Although it is true that practice has viewed the adoption of school policies as being the board's sole responsibility and the implementation of administrative regulations as the responsibility of the school superintendent and professional staff, the fact is that school officials have no legal authority within themselves for determining administrative regulations. Most state statutes clearly specify that school policies and regulations are within the responsibility of the school board. When the school superintendent and professional staff draft a school district's administrative regulations, they seek such approval from the school board.

THE DEVELOPMENT AND IMPLEMENTATION OF SCHOOL DISTRICT POLICIES AND ADMINISTRATIVE REGULATIONS

The development of a viable list of school policies and accompanying administrative regulations is an arduous task at best. This, perhaps, is why the large majority of school districts in America purchase their school policies and regulations from sources such as the National School Boards Association. Although NSBA does a commendable job of drafting school policy manuals, we do not support this common practice. We submit that purchasing a package of school policies results in two important problems. First, involvement in educational decisions is a major concern of professional administrators and teachers. Is there a better way to engage school personnel in school decisions and operations than having a role to play in determining school district policy and/or the accompanying administrative regulations?

Second, if a school teacher or even a school principal is given a copy of the NSBA policy manual, it most likely will be collecting dust on the bookshelf. The lack of opportunity to be engaged in the development of policy and regulation manuals virtually eliminates any personal commitment to implementing its contents. Rather than being "our product," the manual is viewed as someone else's product.

We commend the work of NSBA in establishing codifying methods for organizing a policy manual. In addition, NSBA has been effective in providing counseling for the development of effective school district policies. Later in this chapter, we demonstrate the NSBA codification system and the Davies-Brickell codification system, which are effective organizational means for school districts to implement. Since policy development is a complex and time-consuming task, school personnel are wise to attack one series of the policy manual at a time. In the following section, we discuss the topics of school policies, administrative regulations, and school rules in detail.

DIFFERENTIATING POLICIES, ADMINISTRATIVE REGULATIONS, AND LAWS

School board policies are specific adaptations to the primary goals that the school district is expected to accomplish. Although the school board is the

only official body that can adopt policies, in practice the school superintendent and sometimes the state legislative branch set forth statements that are
incorporated into the district's policy manual. Policies serve to answer the
question regarding what it is that the school district intends to accomplish. It
is becoming more common for school policies to include verbatim clauses
from state statutes. This practice is due to the fact that all too often the court
sets aside matters such as teacher dismissal, student hearings, and due process procedures because the specific procedures within the state statute were
violated.

School board policies differ from administrative regulations in several
ways. For example, school policies are concerned with aims and objectives
as opposed to administrative procedures. An effective policy leaves room for
the administrative discretion on the part of the school superintendent and
professional staff. It is common for policies to assign responsibilities for
implementation to the school superintendent and other members of the professional staff.

School boards are viewed as extensions of the state legislature and thus
are legal entities. Boards have the right to adopt school policies as long as
they do not adversely contradict state statutes or federal laws. Policy statements are general in nature and refer to an area of primary importance to the
citizenry. Another feature of a school policy is that it commonly is applicable
for a long period of time. That is, although related administrative procedures
for implementing a policy might change, a policy is likely to remain in place.
As previously noted, an effective policy serves to answer the question, "What
is the school district to do?"

On the other hand, an *administrative regulation* answers the question,
"How to do it?" How can an administrative regulation be identified? Besides
the fact that it centers on the foregoing question, it is a specific statement(s)
that focuses on the procedures that will be implemented to reach the expectations of a stated policy. While school policies are legislative in nature, administrative regulations are executive statements. Regulations are specific
and leave little room for administrative discretion.

Administrative regulations theoretically do not have to be approved by
the school board, although wise school administrators commonly do so. It
should be clear, of course, that the authority to draft administrative regulations is an authority delegated to the school superintendent by the school
board. Asking the school board to review administrative regulations carries
with it several positive outcomes. First of all, a manual of effective administrative regulations presented to the school board demonstrates accountability
and shows that the school leaders are doing their job administratively in
implementing the board's policies. Second, examination of the school district's administrative regulations provides an opportunity to "test" if the
school board and professional staff are "on the same page" relative to a

policy at hand. Third, school board members commonly do have questions about procedures and can give beneficial suggestions for improving regulation statements.

JUST FOR THE FUN OF IT!

Take a few minutes to identify each of the following entries as a policy, an administrative regulation, or a bylaw. Circle each entry as P (policy), R (regulation), or BL (bylaw).

1. No school board standing committee shall be appointed to perform any of the Board's functions. P, R, BL
2. All capital property owned by the school district and valued at $1,000 or more will be inventoried annually. P, R, BL
3. Appropriate reports will be submitted to the Board on a regular basis to assist Board members in carrying out the affairs of the school district. P, R, BL
4. Local purchasing will be favored whenever the following factors are equal between local and nonlocal vendors. P, R, BL
5. Sexual harassment by and of employees of the school district is prohibited. P, R, BL
6. An aggrieved employee should directly inform the person engaged in sexually harassing conduct or communicate that such conduct or communication is offensive and must stop. P, R, BL
7. Employee suspension and dismissal shall be in accordance with the laws of the state. P, R, BL
8. It is the responsibility of the school superintendent and persons delegated by that office to determine staffing needs of the school district and to recruit/select qualified applicants to recommend to the school board. P, R, BL
9. Don't shoot until you see the whites of their eyes. P, R, BL
10. Don't shoot until you have a sure shot. P, R, BL

We view foregoing statements as illustrative rather than examples of quality policy, regulation, or bylaw statements. Only entry 1 is a bylaw. It states a specific way in which the school board will carry out its function. Entries 4, 6, 7, and 9 are administrative regulations. Each entry stipulates a specific procedure that is to be followed. Entries 2, 3, 5, 8, and 10 are policies. Entry 5 establishes what is to be expected regarding sexual harassment. Entry 9 is a regulation since it gives a specific procedure regulating the time when a person is to shoot. Entry 10, however, leaves room for the shooter's discretion regarding the best time to shoot.

EXAMPLES OF SCHOOL POLICIES AND ACCOMPANYING ADMINISTRATION REGULATIONS

Consider the following policy statement: Example #1.

JBAB Corporal Punishment

Believing in positive strategies relative to student discipline, corporal punishment is prohibited in the Lafayette County School District. No employee of the school district or volunteer, intern, or visiting person may use corporal punishment for disciplinary purposes in the case of any student. The school board defines corporal punishment as any form of physical abuse including spanking, paddling, slapping, or any other form of physical abuse.

JBABA

School personnel are not prohibited from using reasonable force to control behavior or to inhibit or remove a person from the scene who is demonstrating unreasonable and/or dangerous behavior on school grounds when necessary.

Consider the following administrative regulation: Example #1.

JBABA Corporal Punishment Guidelines within the Local School:

School district policy JBABA permits the use of reasonable force to control behavior or to inhibit or remove a person from the scene who is demonstrating unreasonable and/or dangerous behavior on or off school grounds when necessary. In implementing this district policy, the following measures/actions will be implemented if and when necessary:

1. To intervene and stop a dangerous situation threatening injury to others
2. For the purposes of self-defense
3. For restraining a person from using a dangerous weapon of any kind
4. For the safety and protection of persons or prohibiting the destruction of property
5. For gaining control of an unruly classroom situation or improper demonstration on or off school grounds
6. For stopping an action by a student that is obviously injurious to himself or herself

Any intervention by any school employee should be based on the fact that the dangerous behavior was present and active. If not an emergency, local security personnel should be contacted to handle the matter at hand.

Consider the following policy statement: Example #2.

4111 Recruitment and Selection

It is the responsibility of the superintendent of schools and persons delegated by him or her to determine the personnel needs of the school district and to locate suitable candidates to recommend to the board. There shall be no discrimination against any applicant or candidate for employment by reason of race, color, national origin, creed, marital status, sex, or age. It shall be the duty to the superintendent of schools to see that persons nominated for employment shall meet all the qualifications established by law and the Board of Education for the type of position for which the nomination is made.

Consider the following administrative regulation: Example #2.

4111 Recruitment and Selection

In the employment of teachers and other instructional personnel, special consideration is given to professional training, teaching experience, and personal characteristics desirable in good teachers. Each applicant will:

1. Complete an official position application and submit a college transcript to the office of human resources.
2. Provide the names of at least three references that are well acquainted with the applicant's work experiences, teaching record, and personal characteristics.
3. Be available for a telephone interview and personal interview(s) if so requested.
4. Present evidence that indicates that he or she is certified/licensed to teach in the state.
5. Have a background check and its results presented to the school superintendent prior to being hired officially by the Board of Education of the school district.

The foregoing policy and regulation examples are not presented as "models" that school districts should implement. Rather, the examples serve to demonstrate the differences between a policy and an administrative regulation. Check the policy statement for the criteria previously noted relative to purpose and specificity. The policy example establishes the school board's purpose of forbidding corporal punishment by any school personnel. It centers on a topic of primary importance and can exist as stated for an extended period of time. It leaves room for the discretionary decisions of the school superintendent and professional staff for its implementation.

The administrative regulation, on the other hand, is quite specific in the accompanying statement as to how employees may act in cases of dangerous situations. When and how the employee can act in emergency cases is set forth with specific examples of intervention procedures. The policy can remain in place, although the procedures might be changed to deal with unseen circumstances and/or implemented to improve intervention procedures.

HOW THE SCHOOL COMMUNITY BENEFITS BY AN EFFECTIVE SET OF SCHOOL POLICIES AND REGULATIONS

Not only does the school district personnel benefit from viable school policies and regulations, but other community stakeholders receive positive outcomes as well. Policies are outcomes of the educational goals that are vested in the culture of community. Policies reveal just how the school's vision is being reflected in the purposes of the school. Viable policy and regulations serve an important legal function for the school board and school district.

Policy development provides meaningful opportunities for the school community to be involved in the decision-making process. Such involvement can enhance the confidence of community members that the educational program of the school district is indeed centering on meaningful purposes and is in the best interests of students.

Viable school policies and regulations serve to establish a basis for intelligent decision making and help to direct decision making at proper levels within the school system. Thus, school policies and regulations serve the purpose of the division of labor between the school board and the school superintendent and administrative staff. They serve to give the school board the control that it needs to direct the aims of the school program and gives the school superintendent and staff more freedom to lead administratively.

Communication is always an issue of importance in the minds of parents and other community members. Effective school policies serve a key role in communicating with the members of the community. Policies serve as important evidence that the school board is tending to the important school goals and purposes that community members view as paramount importance.

Of course, the community's electorate commonly elects school board members. The board represents the legislative body of the school district. On the other hand, administrative regulations are the responsibility of the school administrators and professional staff. They represent the executive branch of the school district. Thus, policies and regulations represent the distinct division of labor between the school board and the professional staff.

As previously mentioned, policy and regulation development can result in improving the communication between the board and personnel in the school district. In addition, effective policies foster the promotion of creativity and release of talent within the school district's personnel. Effective policies allow for the use of professional discretion on the part of effective school leaders. Those persons that participate in the development and implementation of policies and procedures gain the opportunity to know the school district, its culture, its strengths, and its needs. Such results lend to the confidence of individuals for making relevant decisions and implementing meaningful educational programs that center on student needs and interests.

HOW TO ORGANIZE SCHOOL POLICIES AND ADMINISTRATIVE REGULATIONS FOR EASY REFERENCE

Just think about a telephone book, dictionary, or school library that did not have an effective system for classifying, organizing, and listing names and phone numbers, words, or books. A new telephone is placed in a home, but how is it included in the telephone book? A new word such as *syntality* is new to the vocabulary—how is it placed in the dictionary? A new science book is ordered the school library—where is it to be placed on the shelf? Assume that a new school district policy is approved by your school board; how is it to be coded in the policy manual?

"When NSBA first obtained the Davies-Brickell classification system in the early 1960s, the organization used this pioneering coding method as a way to encourage school districts to commit their policies to written form" (NSBA, 1991, p. 1). Since the development of policy codification systems by the National School Boards Association (NSBA) and by Davies-Brickell (1988), other similar codifications systems have been implemented nationally. The following section describes several codification systems in place today in school districts in America. The NEPN/NSBA system certainly is the most common system for coding policies and regulations nationally.

NEPN/NSBA is an alpha system that uses twelve major classifications/series from A to L as follows:

A. Foundation and Basic Commitments
B. Board Governance and Operations
C. General School Administration
D. Fiscal Management
E. Support Services
F. Facilities Development
G. Personnel
H. Negotiations
I. Instructional Program
J. Students
K. School Community Relations
L. Education Agency Relations

For each major classification, there are subclassifications, divisions, subdivisions, and items. For example, assume that the major classification was students, the first subclassification was discipline, the second division was discipline procedures, and the third subdivision was corporal punishment. The code would be JABC. That is, J is the major classification, A is the first letter of the alphabet and inserted for the first subclassification, B is the second letter of the alphabet and inserted for the second division, and C is the third letter of the alphabet and is inserted for the third subdivision. If there was one entry under the third subdivision of corporal punishment, such as "teacher self-defense," the letter A would be the first item and would be added to the code so as to read JABCA. The fact that this system uses as many as twenty-six letters of the alphabet has the advantage of being more expandable and eliminates the use of decimal points that might tend to increase the possibility of errors in copying and filing.

As previously noted, the NEPN/NSBA codification system is undoubtedly the most frequently used policy system in America's schools.

It is not possible here to show a complete listing for even one major classification of the NEPN/NSBA system. However, the presentation of the first twelve entries for the major classification of personnel is shown below to illustrate how the codification system is applied.

Section G Personnel

GA Personnel Goals/Priority Objectives
GAA Evaluation of Personnel Systems
GB General Personnel Policies
GBA Open Hiring/Equal Employment Opportunity and Affirmative Action
GBAA Sexual Discrimination and Harassment
GBAB Pay Equity
GBB Staff Involvement in Decision Making
GBC Staff Compensation
GBCA Merit/Performance Pay Programs
GBD Communications with Staff (also BHC)
GBE Staff Rights and Responsibilities
GBEA Staff Ethics/Conflict of Interest
GBEB (continued entries)

The Davies-Brickell Codification System differs from the NEPN/NSBA system in that it uses a numerical code as opposed to an alpha code. Thus, the system includes nine major classifications/series as follows:

1000 Community Relations
2000 Administration
3000 Business and Noninstructional Operations
4000 Personnel

5000 Students
6000 Instruction
7000 Construction
8000 Internal Board Policies
9000 Bylaws of the Board

The nine major classifications/series are accompanied appropriately by subclassifications, divisions, subdivisions, items, and subitems. Thus, the code 5134.9 refers to the major classification 5000 (students), the first subclassification, the third division, the forth subdivision, and the ninth item within the classification. The coding system is applied to both the school district's policies and to the administrative regulations. Such a numerical system is used by school districts due to its appropriate classifications and because it is easy to understand and update. This system's one limitation is the fact that any one entry is limited to nine additions (e.g., if the code 5134.9 needed an additional item, entering the number 10 would not work).

Consider the administrative regulation under the major classification of personnel. The third subclassification within the major classification is that of certificated personnel. The first division within the subclassification is that of certificated personnel positions, the first subdivision within the first division is classroom personnel positions, and the second item within the first subdivision is teacher aides. The appropriate code for this entry would be 4311.2.

Figure 1.4 is an abbreviated example of the Personnel (Series 4000) for the Davies-Brickell codification system. The Davies-Brickell personnel series contains an approximate listing of two hundred entries. Only the first thirty-five entries of the series are shown in figure 1.4.

1. Professional...4100
   A. Permanent Personnel..4110
      1. Recruitment and Selection..4111
      2. Appointment..4112
         a. Contract...4112.1
         b. Personnel Records...4112.2
         c. Oaths...4112.3
         d. Orientation...4112.4
      3. Certification...4113
      4. Conditions of Employment..4114
         a. Health Examination..4114.1
         b. Security Check...4114.2
         c. Credit Check..4114.4
      5. Assignment and Transfer...4115
         a. Load/Scheduling..4115.1
         b. Promotion/Demotion...4115.2
      6. Rights, Responsibilities and Duties....................................4116
         a. Civil and Legal Rights...4116.1
            (1) Nondiscrimination...4116.11
            (2) Freedom of Speech..4116.12
         b. Professional Responsibilities..4116.2
            (1) Academic Freedom...4116.21
            (2) Code of Ethics...4116.22
            (3) Teacher Conduct and Dress....................................4116.23
         c. Duties...4116.3
            (1) Teachers..4116.31
            (2) Special Teachers..4116.32
            (3) Librarians..4116.33
            (4) Nurses...4116.34
            (5) Coaches..4116.35
      7. Probation and Evaluation...4117
      8. Tenure...4118
      9. Separation..4119
         a. Retirement...4119.1

Figure 1.4.   Abbreviated Example of the Personnel Series for the Davies-Brickell System. Source: D.R. Davies & H.M. Brickell (1988). An Instructional Handbook on How to Develop School Board Policies, Bylaws, and Administrative Regulations. Naco, AZ: Authors

OTHER EXAMPLES OF POLICY AND REGULATION CODIFICATION SYSTEMS

Clark County School District Policy Manual—Osceola, Iowa

The policy manual used by the Clark County School District in Iowa is organized according to a numeric codification system. There are nine major classifications with subclassifications, divisions, and subdivisions similar to the Davies-Brickell system. However, the Clark County School District policy system includes a unique and most valuable component. For example, the system uses four signs or symbols to differentiate a policy and an administrative regulation. The letter R is used to indicate that a statement is an administrative regulation rather than a school board policy. The letter E is inserted after a policy code to signify that the statement is an exhibit rather than a board policy. The words *Legal Reference* tells the reader where they can find the statutes, case law, attorney general opinion, or administrative rule that provides the authority for the policy. When a policy relates to another policy in the policy manual, the term *cross reference* is inserted to help the user find related policies in the manual.

In the introduction to the policy manual, it is emphasized that each person holding a manual has the responsibility of keeping the manual current as new policies are adopted and/or revised. It is quite evident that the school district's board of directors and administrative leaders view the development and implementation of policy development as a dynamic, ongoing process. Interestingly enough, inquiries about the school policies in the manual may be directed to the board members or to the superintendent by telephone or in writing.

EXAMPLES OF CODIFICATION SYSTEMS IMPLEMENTED IN VARIOUS SCHOOL DISTRICTS

Harvard County Public Schools, Bel Air, Maryland

The Harvard County Public Schools uses twelve major policy classifications: Students, Instruction, School Management, Safety and Security, Stakeholders, Ethics, Personnel, Fiscal, Contracting and Procurement, District Management, School System Governance and Equity, and Nondiscrimination. The classifications of safety and security, stakeholders, equity and nondiscrimination, and contracting and procurement appear to be somewhat different than the one used by the NEPN/NSBA and Davies-Brickell systems.

The coding example that was examined also used a different numbering pattern. For the first subclassification of student attendance, the number 0001-000 is used. For the second subclassification of age of entrance, the number 0002-000 is used. The number 0003-000 is use for the third subclassification of admission policy.

Coding System for Baltimore County Public Schools

The Baltimore County Public Schools uses major classifications (series) quite similar to those of the Davies-Brickell system. However, the system's subclassifications are quite different. Two of the Baltimore major classifications and their subclassifications are shown below.

Major Series

- Students (5000)
- Subseries—Students 5000

- Student Resources 5001
- BCPS 1 5002
- Student Handbook 5003
- Course Registration Guide 5004
- Lunch Menus 5005
- Service Learning 5006

Subseries—Administration 2000

- Board of Education 2001
- Superintendent 2002
- Assistant Superintendents 2003
- Superintendent's Cabinet 2004
- Blueprint 2.0 2005
- Master Plan 2006

Our concern centers on the premise that knowledge of public school law is of paramount importance, and the fact "that many classroom teachers and administrators regarded legal principles applicable to public education with apathy or disinterest" (Lynch & Kuehl, 1983, p. 168). Empirical evidence makes it clear that all school personnel must be competent and well acquainted with the nature and importance of local school policies and regulations as well as the legislation and court decisions that affect their daily work as teachers and administrators.

Williams (2015) points out, "Education is so important to our society that it's a massive area for the law. . . . But since education is in the vortex of hundreds of billions of dollars of spending, plus political and governmental differences, plus people's dearly guarded sovereignty over their children, you bet there are going to be a lot of court cases involving education" (p. 1).

School leaders and teachers do not need to serve as "school lawyers," but they do need to be knowledgeable of legal sources and then be wise relative to the implications of conditions and situations that often result in court cases. Knowing what has been said about what can and cannot be done in certain instances serves school personnel well in avoiding trouble spots that are confronted almost on a daily basis. Students, parents, and teachers are able to present many occasions when a school leader can act unwisely or fail to act wisely due to lack of legal knowledge. This point underscores the primary reason that many court cases are reviewed in this book. It isn't just that a specific court case provides specific information about school law but that the cases represent the kinds of major issues/problems that are faced by school leaders and suggest "red flags" that school leaders need to be aware of in their daily operations.

Snapshot #1—Administrative Regulations Are Just That, Regulations for Us to Develop and Implement

Superintendent Anderson formed a representative school committee to consider the development of administrative regulations for a newly adopted board policy on student discipline. The board policy centered on the concept that student discipline should be viewed as a positive concern in that student learning from the discipline "problem" should be of utmost importance. In addition, corporal punishment was to be forbidden as a discipline measure unless the teacher and/or other persons were in danger or were using it for the purpose of self-defense.

Superintendent Anderson opened the first meeting of the committee by welcoming the committee members and distributing copies of the school board's new policy on student discipline.

"I do wish that the school board had included us in the decision to prohibit corporal punishment. Board members do not have to be in our schools every day to witness what goes on and what we have to contend with regarding student control and disrespect. Just yesterday a smart aleck junior told me that I would have to put the rubber hose away and treat him as he wanted to be treated," opined one school principal in attendance.

Olivia Charleston, elementary school principal, commented, "It isn't just what goes on in the middle and high schools in our district. Just last week a sixth-grade teacher told a boy to get back to his desk, sit down and be quiet. The boy replied, 'Make me!' What is a teacher to do? If the teacher does nothing, control just gets worse. If the teacher puts her hands on the student and drags him back to his desk, it seems to be viewed as unnecessary brutality. It's a lose-lose situation."

"Using the hose as corporal punishment might not be the best discipline measure in the secondary school grades," stated Emory Hassinger, physical education teacher and football coach in one of the senior high schools. "It's getting a bit more difficult to get the best effort out of students in our sports programs today. Our assistant football coach gave one of our players fifty pushups for mouthing vulgar terms on the practice field. His dad called me yesterday threatening a lawsuit for unreasonable punishment."

"Well, folks," said Superintendent Anderson. "Let's keep in mind that we have been asked to draft the administrative regulations for the discipline policy and so the control is in our hands. I think that we can be creative in this regard and leave the door open for teacher and administrator discretion on these kinds of disciplinary matters. So, let's roll up our sleeves and get to work."

Consider the matter described in Snapshot 1 and then take a few minutes to consider your position on the situation as a member of the committee. Then examine the five possible actions/behaviors of committee members and select the one response to your present disposition. Avoid answers such as "I will seek additional information," "I wouldn't select any of the five entries," or "I will just sit back and wait for a good time to state recommendations on this matter." After making your choice among the five possible actions, write one or two paragraphs that support your selection.

In writing your brief response, assume that you are reporting back to the members of the committee. (Note: If this is being considered by a classroom of students, have several students read their choices and have an open discussion on this feedback. Then ask the question: "What must be done to meet the legal requirements that are facing the school district, and what must be done in the best interests of the students?")

Choices:

1. I would support Superintendent Anderson's position to keep in mind that the committee is in control of the administrative regulations and we have a great opportunity to draft recommended regulations that favor our thinking as to how policy matters on student discipline should be attended in our schools.
2. Superintendent Anderson's position on the task lacks the focus that is needed to draft effective administrative regulations. I am in favor of taking more time to discuss the status of student behavior in our schools and what is needed to either retain the present conditions or improve them.
3. I would volunteer to examine the current state statutes on school discipline and corporal punishment and report back to the committee before we take any time to actually draft regulations until we all are better informed about the legal status of the topic at hand.
4. I came into the teaching profession thinking that teaching is what I was going to do. If I have to spend my time in the classroom trying to keep order with a class of students that keeps telling me that "they have the freedom of speech" and "what they are wearing is disruptive only to me and not to class members," then I want to leave the profession.
5. Come on now, let's get on with it. You know as well as I that whatever we recommend will be changed by the administration and then by the school board to suit their views on the topic. Either that or the school board will turn the matter over to some state educators' association and they will send back "boilerplate" recommendations that sound great for public relations purposes.

KEY IDEAS AND RECOMMENDATIONS SET FORTH IN CHAPTER 1

The following entries are viewed as the key ideas and recommendations discussed in chapter 1.

- *Vital Importance of Legal Knowledge Base*: Educational leaders are increasingly in a position in which knowledge of school law looms important. Knowledge of the laws of the land is foundational for the leader's ability to provide proper supervision and protect the rights of faculty and student personnel. Yet studies have found that there is a lack of knowledge on the part of school leaders relative to the legality of situations that they face on a daily basis.
- *The U.S. Constitution Is the Supreme Law of the Land*: All other government agencies and legal courts are inferior to rulings of the Supreme Court.
- *School Leaders Work in a Legal World*: The public schools in America operate in a culture shaped by legal decisions. To be a professional leader in education, one cannot escape the need to know the laws that affect positive change.
- *The Basis for Federal Support for Education*: Public education in America is a federal concern, but it should not be a federal function. The statements that we can have federal monetary support without having federal control has not been in evidence historically.
- *The Basis for State's Responsibility for Education*: Amendment X of the U.S. Constitution reserves powers to states for matters not specifically delegated to the federal government or prohibited to the states or to the people. Education is not mentioned in the Constitution, and therefore it is assumed to be a state responsibility. County and local school districts are creatures of the state legislatures, and therefore county and local school boards are legislative bodies responsible to state control.
- *Freedom for All*: Major constitutional amendments such as Amendment I and Title VII are responsible to state control. NDEA has established limitations on Congress regarding prohibiting the rights of American citizens. Freedom of speech and the press, peaceable assembly, and the right to petition for redress of grievances set forth the foundation for many rights that students and teachers enjoy today. Nondiscrimination clauses in Title VII have been far reaching in protecting the equal rights of all citizens of the United States.
- *School Leaders Are Inextricably Tied to a Legal World*: The school leader today, in order to be effective, must be effectively involved in the development and implementation of school policies, administrative regulations, and local school rules. School leaders must be informed about school

district policies and administrative regulations for effective decision-making practices. Such knowledge serves to help the school leader think responsibly before a decision is made and to provide effective supervision of teachers and students and to protect the rights of both student and faculty personnel.

- *Effective School Policies and Administrative Regulations Lead to a Win-Win Result*: Everyone benefits by having an effective manual of school district policies and administrative regulations. Policies give the school board the control that it wants to establish the goals/objectives of the school program, and administrative regulations give school leaders the ability to use their creative talents in providing the procedures for accomplishing the goals and objectives set forth by the school board.

DISCUSSION QUESTIONS

1. Assume that you have just been named as the new principal of Wymore Middle School. This is your first administrative position as a principal. In a conversation with another principal in the school district, you ask him about the importance of having legal knowledge in the principal's role. He responds, "I don't really worry about it, the school district retains an attorney to take care of those matters." What are your thoughts about the principal's response to your question?
2. Differentiate between a court ruling and a state statute, as these activities affect a school administrator's responsibilities.
3. You plan to address the school's teachers and classified personnel on the topic of the school's legal responsibilities. Make a brief outline of the major points that you will make when speaking to the school employees.
4. Group Activity: Divide the group into teams of four persons. Have teams assume the pro or con position and debate the proposition: "The federal government has violated the historical principle that education is a national concern."
5. What types of educational court cases do you visualize coming before the U.S. Supreme Court in the future?

CASE STUDIES

Case 1.1 That's the Last Straw! Or Is It?

The school attendance clerk was calling homes and checking on student absences. When she contacted Mrs. Robertson, mother of Elsie, a senior student in the high school, she asked why Elsie was not in school that day.

Mrs. Robertson responded, "Elsie is not feeling well today and might not be back to school tomorrow either."

"Just what is her problem?" asked the attendance clerk. "Elsie has been absent four days over the last two weeks. Has she seen a physician?"

"Well, yes," said Mrs. Robertson. "The doctor said that Elsie is pregnant. But the doctor said that it would be OK for her to attend school."

"Well, wait just a minute. Let me get back to you on this matter, Mrs. Robertson. I'll have to check this out with Principal Manuel. He might recommend homeschooling for Elsie. I'll get back as soon as possible. Goodbye."

The attendance clerk went to Principal Manuel's office and reported the results of her phone call to Mrs. Robertson.

"What does she mean when she says Elsie will be back to school? Not if I can help it," said Principal Manuel. "All we need is a pregnant girl walking around the school halls. I will report this matter to the Superintendent's office, but then I will check to see about homeschooling arrangements. Problems, problems. What in the world will be next? I thought that I had seen it all."

Discussion: Take a few minutes to think about what you would do at this time if you were in the position of school principal in this case. Does Principal Manuel appear to be following up appropriately? Keep your response well in mind. Later, in chapter 4, the topic of student pregnancy is discussed in detail.

Case 1.2 Let's Have the State's Attorney General Decide This Matter

In a meeting of the school principals of Northeast Lafayette School District, the matter of teacher illegal substance abuse came to the floor. Superintendent Burnett had recommended the suspension of a high school teacher when he was arrested for having an illegal substance in his automobile.

"We simply cannot allow our teachers to be involved with illegal drugs and then try to be effective in the classroom with students," commented Superintendent Burnett. "I have recommended suspension in this case and will recommend the teacher's dismissal at the next executive meeting of the school board."

Ricardo Mendez, an elementary school principal in the Northeast Lafayette School District, raised his hand and was allowed to speak.

"Well, Dr. Burnett," stated Mendez. "Isn't there a matter of due process in these cases? I for one am not clear as to what our school policy says in cases of this kind."

"We know that the police have cited this teacher for possessing illegal drugs and he was found guilty in a court of law," responded Superintendent Burnett. "Two board members have called me on this matter and both were extremely upset. Each asked what we plan to do regarding this unfortunate occurrence affecting our school district's reputation. Our school district's policy is clear in these matters. The use of illegal drugs by students and employees is prohibited. I am trying to keep a low profile on this case for the good of the reputation of our school district. Nevertheless, I have asked the state's attorney general to give me an opinion on this matter. His opinion will serve us well in bringing this case to a close."

Discussion: What are your thoughts regarding Case 1.2? There are several legal considerations that are prevalent in this case. We begin by considering Superintendent Burnett's decision to ask the state's attorney general to give his opinion on this matter. We could argue that this was not a responsible action on his part since suspension and teacher dismissal becomes a responsibility of the school board. Nevertheless, although a state attorney general commonly is authorized to issue official opinions to school officials on legal matters related to their work responsibilities, such an opinion cannot be a legal ruling that would "close" the case for Superintendent Burnett.

The attorney general's opinion might serve to avoid legal liability for his or her actions, unless an appropriate court acts on such a case and finds that decision was legally incorrect. In addition, courts acting on similar cases have ruled that unless the teacher's drug behavior can be shown to interrupt and/or inhibit his or her ability to perform effectively the classroom, dismissing the teacher is not appropriate. Of course, the activities of due process loom important in such cases as well. That is, the school officials must show or have proof that the incident had adverse effects on the students' educational program of the school. Convincing proof of the adverse effects is of special importance.

REFERENCES

Davies, D. R., & Brickell, H. M. (1988). *An instructional handbook on how to develop school board policies, by-laws,* and *administrative regulations*. Naco, AZ: Daniel R. Davies, pp. 9–12.

Hasbrouck v. School Committee of Bristol, 46 R.I., 466 (1925).

Lynch, H. Lewis, & Kuehl, R. (1983). Recent graduates have definite ideas on how to improve teacher education programs. *Teacher Evaluator* 59, 168–72.

National School Boards Association. (1991). The school administrator's guide to the NEPN/ NSBA policy development system. Alexandria, VA: Author.

Norton, M. S. (1969). *Federal aid for education: The bulletin of the National Association of Secondary School Principals* 43, 248.

Peterson, L. J., Rossmiller, R. A., & Volz, M. M. (1978). *The law and public school operation*. New York: Harper & Row Publishers, Inc.

Tiedt, S. W. (1966). *The role of the federal government in education*. New York: Oxford University Press, Inc.

Williams, S. D. (2015). Parental involvement: Legal issues, famous court cases. *Show and Tell for Parents*. http://www.showandtellforparents.com/wfdata/frame154-1000/pressrel64.asp

Chapter Two

The Legal Rights and Liabilities of School Principals

Primary chapter goal: To examine the legal rights, responsibilities, and liabilities of school principals and other school leaders concerning what they need to know in order to be effective in their leadership roles.

> In truth, public school officials must be ever mindful of legal considerations. From school funding to treatment of religion, from equity concerns to discipline, from curriculum possibilities to actions that might be prohibited, the law has a say—and a sway—over how school board members and educators do their jobs. (Center for Public Education, 2006)

We reviewed the legislative statutes of one state and found no references to the school principal. Yet this school leader must deal daily with his or her own school personnel, parents, students, and a variety of individuals within the school community. These relationships commonly are saturated with policies, administrative regulations, state legislation, federal laws, and court rulings that have direct effects on the principal's decision-making and professional behavior. Each chapter of this book holds specific implications for the legal responsibilities of school principals. Although chapter 3 and chapter 4 focus on the rights of teachers and students respectively, federal laws, state statutes, and court cases for teachers and students commonly have implications for the school principal as well.

It is important to keep in mind that court cases are always ongoing within the fifty states. The differences of court rulings continue to evolve, and a case ruled on one occasion for the plaintiff might well be reversed later by another more superior court. We note reversals in several court cases studied. Of special notice were reversals in appeal courts related to cases on classified personnel. "Support personnel typically constitute 30%–50% of the total school district staff" (Norton, 2008, p. 371). Increasingly, the school principal is involved in the supervision, development, and evaluation of support personnel assigned to his or her school.

WHAT LEGAL ISSUES AND PROBLEMS DO PRACTICING SCHOOL PRINCIPALS VIEW AS MOST SERIOUS?

A survey of elementary, middle, and secondary school principals, supported by the Emeritus College of Arizona State University, was administered in 2015 that focused on the most serious and time-consuming legal issues/ problems that they faced. Part 1 of the survey centered on information relating to the time being spent on legal matters and the participants' views of the adequacy of their preparation program for dealing effectively with the legal world in which they must operate. Part II reveals the participants' perceptions of the "seriousness" of a comprehensive listing of potential issues and problems facing the school principal in relations to students, teachers/staff, and related legal matters that are encountered in this leadership role. Figure 2.1 sets forth the questions posed and the responses received from the participants.

As noted in the principal survey that follows, the primary purposes of the survey were to identify the nature of the legal issues and problems being encountered by practicing school principals and to gain knowledge as to those legal issues that were "most troublesome" for them in meeting their position responsibilities. Information revealed by the principals' responses was viewed as being significant for identifying the legal content best suited for preparation and in-service administrator programs.

As established by the data collected from the principals' survey, only 5.4 percent of the participants viewed themselves as being "well prepared" for the legal issues and problems that were facing them on the job. Sixteen percent of the participating school principals was of the opinion that they were "not well prepared" to deal with the various legal matters encountered in the leadership role. Most school leaders viewed themselves as being "somewhat prepared" by their administrative preparation programs to deal with the legal matters that they encountered in the position.

The survey included school principals from the elementary, middle, and secondary school levels. Thus, the relativity of the legal questions relating to such matters as student pregnancy, student sexuality issues, student press issues, order of student protection, mandatory reporting of child abuse, and others would tend to differ among the various grade levels. The word *serious* is commonly viewed as being important, grave, significant, or weighty. We further defined the term *serious* in regard to the time requirements, conflict difficulties, quality of impact on relationships, workload, and levels of consternation resulting from the factor of dealing with the various legal issues and problems encountered in the role.

Figure 2.1 presents the survey study instrument that was administered. You might find it interesting and beneficial to complete the survey yourself. Many of the study results are set forth in the content following figure 2.1. You would be able to compare your entries with many of the resulting study statistics.

ARIZONA SCHOOL PRINCIPALS' SURVEY

The Legal World of the School Principal

Introduction: We are asking selected Arizona school principals to provide their thoughts on the nature of the legal responsibilities facing school leaders. The results of the survey will be reported to the Arizona School Administrators Association and university personnel that prepare school administrators, and ultimately Rowman & Littlefield of Lanham, Maryland, will publish them in a national publication. The study is supported by Arizona State University Emeritus College, and the results will be distributed to the several Arizona administrator programs and associations that prepare school leaders. All data received will be considered as part of the group data. We will not have the resources to follow up with a second request, so please complete the survey now and return it in the enclosed self-addressed, stamped envelope. Your help with this project is appreciated.

Part 1 — Status of Your Legal Responsibilities as a School Leader

1. Please give your best estimate of the time you spend during the year on matters that hold implications relative to student rights, teacher rights, parent rights, and other related legal responsibilities. Consider, of course, the highly significant matters of teacher dismissal, student suspension, special needs students, testing requirements, teacher evaluation, student searches, social media (cell phones), faculty dress, sex issues, and student/teacher discipline.
2. Circle the estimated time spent on legal matters during the school year.

   a. 0% to 5% of my total time
   b. 6% to 10% of my total time
   c. 11% to 15% of my total time
   d. 16% to 20% of my total time
   e. More than 20% of my total time

3. How well were you prepared in your administrator preparation program to deal with the various legal matters facing you as school principal?

   a. Well prepared
   b. Somewhat prepared
   c. Not well prepared

4. What primary resources do you use to keep abreast or seek advice on legal matters encountered in your position responsibilities? Circle each entry that applies.

   a. Legal resources available within the jurisdiction of the school district (district office, legal counsel, school district's legal counsel)
   b. Legal resources available from other administrative colleagues
   c. Legal resources available through professional memberships in state organizations
   d. Personal reading/research on legal requirements including court cases/rulings
   e. Other resources:_____

5. How would you rank the seriousness of legal issues/problems that you face as school principal with other major position responsibilities that you encounter, such as curriculum development, staff professional development, planning/organization, coordinating, communication, and budgeting?

   I would rank the legal issues/problems:

   a. Among the most serious issues/problems that I encounter in the role of principal
   b. Among the somewhat serious issues/problems that I encounter in the role of principal
   c. Among the less serious issues/problems that I encounter in the role of principal

Part II—Identification of the Primary Issues/Problems Facing Local School Principals

Part II sets forth several potential legal issues/problems being encountered by school principals today. For each entry, *check its level of seriousness* (e.g., serious, difficult but less serious, or not serious) in regard to the factors of time requirements, conflicts, relationships, workload, and consternation in your role as school principal. Please note that the following sections emphasize issues/problems related to students, teachers/staff personnel, and other principal-related legal issues/problems.

LEGAL ISSUE/PROBLEM	SERIOUS	DIFFICULT BUT LESS SERIOUS	NOT SERIOUS
a. Students' Rights	_____	_____	_____
b. Free Speech by Students	_____	_____	_____
c. Student Dress Code	_____	_____	_____
d. Corporal Punishment	_____	_____	_____
e. Student Suspension	_____	_____	_____
f. Drug Violations	_____	_____	_____
g. Cyberbullying	_____	_____	_____
h. Special Student Needs	_____	_____	_____
i. Student Hearings	_____	_____	_____
j. Student Searches	_____	_____	_____
k. Student Discipline	_____	_____	_____
l. Mandatory Reporting	_____	_____	_____
m. Sexual Conduct	_____	_____	_____
n. Pregnancy	_____	_____	_____
o. Gender Identification	_____	_____	_____
p. Student Admissions	_____	_____	_____
q. Student Placement	_____	_____	_____
r. Student Grading	_____	_____	_____
s. Drug Testing	_____	_____	_____
t. Student Clubs	_____	_____	_____
u. Student Press Issues	_____	_____	_____
v. Student Homework Issues	_____	_____	_____
w. Student Immunizations	_____	_____	_____

Legal Issues/Problems Related to Students

x. Student Due Process   _____   _____   _____

y. Student Attendance   _____   _____   _____

z. Smart Snacks Regulations FERPA _____   _____   _____

aa. Social Media (cell phones)   _____   _____   _____

bb. Student Sexuality Issues   _____   _____   _____

cc. Transgender Students   _____   _____   _____

Please list other student legal issues/problems

dd.   _____   _____   _____

ee.   _____   _____   _____

ff.   _____   _____   _____

LEGAL ISSUES/PROBLEMS RELATED TO TEACHER/STAFF PERSONNEL

a. Teacher Insubordination   _____   _____   _____

b. Teacher Dismissal   _____   _____   _____

c. Teacher Evaluation   _____   _____   _____

d. Teacher Incompetency   _____   _____   _____

e. Teacher Neglect of Duty   _____   _____   _____

f. Teacher Tenure   _____   _____   _____

g. Breach of Contract   _____   _____   _____

h. Teacher Absenteeism   _____   _____   _____

i. Student Relations (disciplinary) _____   _____   _____

j. Teacher/Student Relations (sexual) _____   _____   _____

Legal Issues/Problems Related to Students (cont'd)

k. Teacher Suspension   _____   _____   _____

l. Teacher Hiring (legal)   _____   _____   _____

m. Teacher Placement   _____   _____   _____

n. Teacher Rights   _____   _____   _____

o. Faculty Dress   _____   _____   _____

p. Teacher Discipline (personal) _____   _____   _____

q. Teacher/Staff Tattoos   _____   _____   _____

r. Teacher/Staff Sexual Orientation _____   _____   _____

Please List Other Teacher/Staff Legal Issues

s.   _____   _____   _____

t.   _____   _____   _____

u.   _____   _____   _____

OTHER PRINCIPAL LEGAL ISSUES/PROBLEMS BEING ENCOUNTERED

a. School Safety Measures   _____   _____   _____

b. Book Selection

c. Handling of School Funds   _____   _____   _____

d. Curriculum Mandates   _____   _____   _____

e. Classified Personnel Issues   _____   _____   _____

f. Religion in Schools   _____   _____   _____

Legal Issues/Problems Related to Students (cont'd)

g. Order of Student Protection   _____   _____   _____

h. Parental Relations   _____   _____   _____

i. Police Searches of Students   _____   _____   _____

j. Use of Tax Credit Money   _____   _____   _____

k. Interview of Students by CPS/DCS   _____   _____   _____

l. Mandatory Reporting of Child Abuse _____   _____   _____

m. Confidential Addresses of Children   _____   _____   _____

n. Custodial Issues   _____   _____   _____

Please List Other Legal Issues/Problems Being Encountered

o.   _____   _____   _____

p.   _____   _____   _____

q.   _____   _____   _____

Legal Issues/Problems Related to Students (cont'd)

Thank you. Please return the completed survey to:
Dr. M. Scott Norton
2075 E. Laguna Dr.
Tempe, AZ 85282
Personal note: I presently serve as professor emeritus of Arizona State University and formerly served as an adjunct professor at Northern Arizona University. In addition, I served as the first president of the Higher Education Division of Arizona School Administrators, Inc.

PRESENTATION OF THE SURVEY STUDY RESULTS

Most Serious Legal Problems as Related to Student Personnel

The leading serious legal issues and problems being encountered by practicing school principals in relation to student personnel, in order, were: special student needs (62.5 percent); cyberbullying (55.4 percent); social media, cell phones (47.5 percent); drug violations (41.1 percent); student suspension (37.5 percent); mandatory reporting (33.3 percent); student discipline (32.1

percent); sexual conduct (32.1 percent); student attendance (30.9 percent); and student sexuality issues (28.6 percent). In addition, each of these matters received high percentage reports as being "difficult but less serious." Note that each of these legal issues is discussed additionally later in this chapter or in other chapters of the book.

As would be expected, those items named by the participating school principals as being most serious were judged not serious by a much smaller percentage. For example, the entry of special student needs, which ranked first as a serious student legal problem, received only 7.1 percent of the responses for being "not serious."

Difficult but less serious legal problems included student grading (54.1 percent); student discipline (52.4 percent); student rights (50.0 percent); student hearings (46.4 percent); student attendance (43.6 percent); student admissions (42.9 percent); student suspension (41.1 percent); student searches (41.1 percent); smart snacks regulations, FERPA (39.6 percent); student placement (39.3 percent); and social media, cell phones (39.0 percent).

Legal Issues and Problems Related to Teacher/Staff Personnel

Teacher evaluation with a serious problem response of 57.1 percent led the "serious legal problems" in the teacher/staff category. In addition, 32.1 percent of the school principals listed evaluation as a difficult but less serious problem. We recommend that the reader secure a copy of the recent book published by Rowman & Littlefield (2016), *The Changing Landscape of School Leadership: Recalibrating the School Principalship*. Bold changes in the perspectives of teacher evaluation are presented in detail in the book. In brief, the requirements for teacher evaluation are altered and replaced by improvement leadership provisions. The school's assistant principal and principal focus on teaching improvement through placing emphasis on coaching and mentoring as opposed to the questionable process of teacher assessment that seldom leads to actual improvement in classroom instruction.

Other serious legal problems in the category of teacher/staff included teacher dismissal (39.2 percent); teacher incompetency (37.9 percent); teacher hiring (legal) (33.9 percent); teacher discipline (personal) (27.6 percent); teacher neglect of duty (27.3 percent); teacher/student relations (sexual) (22.8 percent); teacher suspension (22.8 percent); teacher insubordination (19.6 percent); and student relations (disciplinary) (14.3 percent). Data reveal that one-third of the participating school principals ranked teacher/student sexual relations as a serious or as a difficult but less serious problem.

We need to keep in mind that the listed percentages do not represent the number of problems that the school leaders have encountered. A school principal might have checked teacher evaluation as being a serious issue/ problem, for example, due to one case only in which a teacher filed a complaint or difficult lawsuit or perhaps checked the entry as serious because of other reasons such as the time that the evaluation process necessitates.

Other Principal Legal Issues/Problems Being Encountered by the School Principal

Curriculum mandates were viewed as either serious or difficult but less serious legal issues/problems by 87.5 percent of the school principals. Other such legal issues/problems viewed at this level of seriousness were school safety measures (78.2 percent); handling of school funds (76.8 percent); custodial issues (70.2 percent); parental relations (69.2 percent); and mandatory reporting of child abuse (67.8 percent). Such results serve to remind us that the school principal now carries a major responsibility in working with the classified staff of the school. In contemporary school districts, classified staff personnel typically constitute 30 percent to 50 percent of the total school district staff (Norton, 2008). In many school districts, the school principal is required to supervise and evaluate the performance of classified staff personnel that work in his or her school. The majority of legal issues/ problems included in the legal survey is discussed in the various chapters of the book.

STATUS OF THE LEGAL RESPONSIBILITIES OF SCHOOL PRINCIPALS

The opening section of the foregoing principals' survey asked four key questions relating to the impact of the legal world in which they work. Question 1 asked the participants to provide their best estimate of the time spent during the school year on matters that hold implications relative to student rights, teacher rights, and other related legal responsibilities. The results of the four questions posed are reported here.

1. Please give your best estimate of the time you spend during the year on matters that hold implications relative to student rights, teacher rights, and other related legal responsibilities.

    a. 0% to 5% of my total time (Response 10.7%)
    b. 6% to 10% of my total time (Response 10.7%)
    c. 11% to 15% of my total time (Response 19.6%)
    d. 16% to 20% of my total time (Response 14.3%)
    e. More than 20% of my total time (Response 44.6%)

2. How well were you prepared in your administrator preparation program to deal with the various legal matters facing you as school principal?

a. Well prepared (Response 5.4%)
b. Somewhat prepared (Response 78.6%)
c. Not well prepared (Response 16.0%)

3. What primary resources do you use to keep abreast or seek advice on legal matters encountered in your position responsibilities? Circle each entry that applies.

a. Legal resources available within the jurisdiction of the school district (district office, legal counsel, school district's legal counsel) (Response 82.1%)
b. Legal resources available from other administrative colleagues (Response 41.1%)
c. Legal resources available through professional memberships in state organizations (Response 44.6%)
d. Personal reading/research on legal requirements including court cases/ rulings (Response 44.6%)

4. How would you rank the seriousness of legal issues/problems that you face as school principal with other major position responsibilities that you encounter such as curriculum development, staff professional development, planning/organization, coordinating, and budgeting?

a. Among the most serious issues/problems that I encounter in the role of principal (Response 42.9%)
b. Among the somewhat serious issues/problems that I encounter in the role of principal (Response 39.3%)
c. Among the less serious issues/problems that I encounter in the role of principal (Response 17.9%)

The foregoing data make it clear that principals devote a considerable amount of their work time on matters that constitute legal implications. Nearly 60 percent of the participating school principals were spending minimally 16 percent of their time on matters with legal implications; approximately 45 percent were giving more than 20 percent of their work time to legal issues and problems.

Only 5.4 percent of the principals were of the opinion that they were well prepared in their preparation programs to deal with the various legal matters facing them in the principal's role. Although the large majority considered themselves to be "somewhat prepared" to handle the legal matters facing them, another 16 percent were "not well prepared" to do so.

School principals that participated in the legal survey used a variety of resources for keeping abreast or seeing advice legally. However, resources within the jurisdiction of their school district were the leading source for gaining legal advice. Nearly half, 42.9 percent, of the school principals viewed legal issues and problems among the most serious matters that they encounter in their leadership role. Only 17.9 percent of the study participants were of the opinion that legal issues/problems were among the less serious matters being encountered in the position.

TIME OUT! THE PRE-CHAPTER QUIZ

We ask that you take a few minutes to complete the following pre-chapter quiz. The quiz conjures up several topics that we discuss later in the chapter. Do not guess the answers to the questions; rather, just move to the next question if you do not know an answer.

Pre-Quiz

1. School principals, like school board members, enjoy immunity from tort liability (legal obligation of one party to a victim as a result of civil wrong or injury). ____T or ____F
2. Constitutional behavior of a school principal as considered by the courts is determined primarily by the fact that his or her behavior:

    a. is specifically set forth in the principal's position description.
    b. is based primarily on the students' overall record.
    c. is determined on opinions gained over a "lengthy" period of time.
    d. is speedy, deliberative, and fair.

3. If a school principal has earned tenure rights as a teacher in the same school district, the person retains the classification of permanent teacher when promoted to the position of principal. ____T or ____F
4. In some states where there are teacher tenure laws, school principals can earn tenure in their administrative position. ____T or ____F
5. Which of the following sources/entities has the primary authority to prescribe what is to be taught in public schools?

    a..the local board of education
    b. the school district superintendent
    c. the school principal
    d. the state board of education
    e. the state legislature
    f. the federal government

6. Knowing that the school principal serves on the front line of educational administration, state statutes have set forth the legal duties of the position in all fifty states. ____T or ____F

7. Since school principals have unreasonable work responsibilities, according to court findings, principals are given immunity from tort liability within the school and on campus environments. ____T or ____F

8. Although courts have given teachers in loco parentis authority in regard to student discipline, school principals do not enjoy the "in place of parents" concept legally. ____T or ____F

9. Corporal punishment has been finally decided by the U.S. Supreme Court. Corporal punishment violates the Civil Rights Acts and is also unconstitutional. ____T or ____F

10. An assistant school principal learned from other students that a student had marijuana in his school locker. The boy refused to open the locker for the assistant principal. The assistant principal searched the locker and did find marijuana. The court upheld the behavior of the assistant principal on the basis that:

    a. the search was reasonable within the facts and circumstances of the case.
    b. the student's previous record of poor discipline was sufficient to believe the student would be guilty.
    c. the search was within the scope of the assistant principal's duties.
    d. the student's refusal to open the locker himself was viewed as insubordination.

11. What restrictions are placed on teachers' purchases for classroom supplies, computers, band uniforms, and other such instructional materials from classroom supply funds?

    a. Commonly, teachers are allowed to expend funds as they deem appropriate.
    b. Such expenditures are to be determined only by the school official appointed by the school board as the district's business official.
    c. Such expenditures take priority over any other expenditures, such as school furniture.
    d. No such fund is legally approved by state statutes or school policy.

12. Does the school principal have the authority to expel a student from school? ____Yes or ____No

13. A school principal with a school district that is receiving federal funds must "search" the school community for students with special needs. ____T or ____F

14. The old adage that "ignorance of the law" is no excuse has been set aside as *nonlogical* in relation to the position of school principal since no such school leader is expected to be a professional lawyer. ____T or ____F

15. Ability grouping for students in public schools is viewed as discrimination and thus ruled as illegal by the courts. ____T or ____F

We will discuss the answers to each of the questions on the pre-chapter quiz and then give additional consideration to the legal world of the school principal.

Question #1—School principals enjoy immunity from tort liability, is false. Courts have ruled that school principals are liable for his or her negligence. Although both teachers and principal stand in place of a parent in carrying their student responsibilities, they nevertheless are expected to exercise care and reasonable insight when planning and implementing student program activities.

Question #2—Constitutional behavior of school principals is viewed by the courts as (d), the principal was speedy, deliberate, and fair. This view underscores the need for the school principal to deal forthrightly with a pending violation and to be fair in gathering the evidence that surrounded the situation. Fairness would include, of course, due process procedures that set forth charges and gave an opportunity for the student to respond.

Question #3—When the principal earns tenure and then is promoted to the position of principal, he or she retains the classification of permanent teacher, is true. That is, if the school principal should return to the classroom in the same school district, he or she would qualify for permanent tenure as a teacher. Some states have tenure for school administrators. In these cases, after serving as principal, retaining tenure as a teacher is handled somewhat differently. For example, the principal might have to serve as a nontenured teacher for one year. If his or her performance is satisfactory after one year, permanent teacher tenure can be restored on the recommendation of the school superintendent.

Question #4—In some states, the fact that a school principal can earn tenure as an administrator is true. In the case of the *Board of Education v. Swan*, however, the state of California decided that principals do not have tenure in that position. The California case was difficult and complex, involving a female teacher that had been a teacher and school principal in the school district for twenty-nine years. In short, she was asked to return to teaching assignments and she failed to do so. The court ruled that the individual did not have tenure as a school principal and that the school board could cancel contracts with the individual at any time.

Question #5—What entry below has the primary authority to prescribe the curriculum that must be taught in public schools? The answer is (e) the state legislature. From a legal standpoint, the legislature of a state is the only body that can prescribe what is to be taught in the school. It is true that state legislatures commonly delegate this authority to local school boards and the courts can disapprove the teaching of certain subjects, best illustrated by the inability to teach religion. In a related example, the state of Arizona approved a statute that high school students had to pass an examination in civics before being eligible for high school graduation. In some cases, schools are required to teach certain subjects by federal agencies if federal funding is to be approved for the school district.

Question #6—State legislatures have set forth the legal description of the duties for school principals in all fifty states, is false. In fact, few state statutes mention the responsibilities expected of school principals. It is true that certain federal regulations have set forth certain responsibilities for school principals if federal funds are to be received. Nevertheless, principal position descriptions have been left to the discretion of local school boards that have delegated the responsibility to the local school superintendent.

Question #7—School principals have immunity from tort liability, is false. It is clear that the school principal is libel for his or her own negligence. Negligence has been defined as the lack of care comparable to what would be expected by a competent person in the same situation. If reasonable care had been taken by the principal before the accident or injury had taken place or there is clear evidence that the injury to another person was unavoidable, the principal would not be held liable. In many cases, foresight on the part of the principal looms important. That is, signs that special care was taken to inform others of possible dangers and ways were taken to avoid the possibility of injury are precautionary measures and would be duly considered by a court.

Question #8—The statement that principals do not enjoy the in loco parentis concept legally, is false. Courts in California and other states have ruled that teachers, vice principals, principals, and other certified personnel are privileged to exercise the same degree of control over students that parents may legally use and are immunized from criminal prosecution when doing so. Once again, cruel and abusive punishment on the part of school officials is always problematic.

Question #9—The statement that corporal punishment violates the civil rights acts and also is unconstitutional, is false. Corporal punishment, unless forbidden or not addressed in state statutes, has been ruled as permissible by several court actions. However, corporal punishment must be administered with caution in that abusive and/or unreasonable punishment that is excessive will likely be the subject of court action. The point to be underscored is that of reasonableness.

Question #10—An assistant principal was told that a student had marijuana in his locker. The assistant principal searched the locker and did find marijuana. The court upheld the locker search on the basis that (a) the search was reasonable in view of the facts and circumstances of the case.

Question #11—What restrictions are placed on teachers' purchase of supplies such as computers, band uniforms, and other materials? Answer (a), commonly teachers are allowed to expend fund for materials as they deem appropriate. The expenditure of school funds for such things as band uniforms has been challenged, and courts have ruled that band is indeed part of a school's educational program and uniforms are part of the material/equipment needed for programs such as marching bands.

Question #12—Does a school principal have the authority to expel a student from school? The answer is no. Only the school board can expel a student, although student suspension is another matter. Expulsion has been defined as the act of depriving a student the right of membership in the school for some violation or offense that renders him or her unworthy of remaining a member of the school. Expulsion is discussed in detail later in chapter 3. Expulsion, however, is only within the authority of the school board unless set forth otherwise in the statutes of the state.

Question #13—In a school district that is receiving federal funding, each school principal is responsible for identifying all students with disabilities within his or her school jurisdiction even if they are not attending public school. This statement is true. This requirement falls within the Individuals with Disabilities Act (IDEA) of 1990. Private schools may not be funded for providing accommodations under IDEA.

Question #14—Ignorance of the law has not been set aside by the courts as an excuse for illegal behavior. Thus, question #14 is false. The answer underscores the importance of school leaders to do their very best to be knowledgeable of the law as related to their work responsibilities.

Question #15—The statement, "Ability grouping for students in public schools is viewed as discrimination and therefore is ruled as illegal by the courts," is false.

In the following section, we describe several other court cases that are encountered by school principals. Following the presentation of these court rulings, we will discuss other aspects of the school principal's work responsibilities and the legal consideration surrounding them.

SELECTED COURT CASES AND/OR LAWS OF CONCERN FOR THE SCHOOL PRINCIPAL

Case #1— *J. S. v. Bethlehem School District* (807 A.2nd 803; Pa. 2002). Student Derogatory Remarks of His Teacher and His Principal

The case centered on the question as to whether the officials of a school district could suspend a student for showing derogatory and offensive images of his school teacher and principal. The student's website images showed what were viewed as derogatory and threatening images of the teacher as well as derogatory comments about the school principal. The school principal suspended the student, and the case was heard by the Pennsylvania high court. The school district contended that the student's website was both highly derogatory and was threatening as well. The student had pictures on the website with the teacher's bloody head and language that he sought a hit man to kill her. The school district argued that the student's illustration on the website did indeed pose a threat and that, furthermore, the website caused considerable disruption to the school's educational program. The defendant school district used several previous court cases to support the claims of educational disruption and the use of lewd and offensive speech. The state court agreed and ruled in favor of the school district in a 6 to 0 ruling.

This case brought about considerable legal discussion because it did deal with a student's freedom of speech and was also "performed" off campus. In addition, the *Tinker v. Des Moines Independent Community School District*, whereby students wore black armbands at school in protest of the Vietnam War, was a more "peaceful" demonstration, and it took place some fifteen years earlier.

Case #2—*Couch v. Wayne Local School District*, United States District Court, Case 1:12-cv-00625-MRAB Doc # 10 (2011)

This lawsuit is another "free speech" case relative to clothing that a student can wear at school. A student wore a T-shirt with the insignia of Ichthys and a slogan saying, "Jesus Is Not a Homophobe."

We looked up several references and believe that the term *Ichthys* is an acronym meaning "Jesus Christ, the Son of God, our Savior." The word *homophobe* is defined as a person who hates or fears homosexual people. The student was threatened with suspension by the school principal. Next semester, the student went back to school, approached the school principal, and asked for permission to wear the T-shirt once again. Again, he was threatened by suspension if he did so. A legal entity corresponds with the school principal pointing out the student's rights to wear the T-shirt under the First Amendment. The school district responded by saying that the message on the student's T-shirt was indecent and was not appropriate under the school's dress code. As a result, a lawsuit was filed under the authorization of the student's mother as *Couch v. Wayne Local School District*.

The court rendered what was termed an agreed judgment in favor of the plaintiff. The defendants were prohibited from disallowing the student to wear the T-shirt and were ordered to pay the plaintiff $20,000 for damages and costs. The ruling barred any further litigation concerning this case. Apparently, this move was set forth as part of the agreed judgment.

Snapshot #2.1 "This Classroom Isn't Big Enough for the Two of Us, Pardner." Law #1—School Sentinel and the Right of School Teachers to Possess Firearms, July 1, 2015

Beginning on July 1, 2015, schoolteachers in South Dakota will be permitted to possess firearms. Certain conditions are required by the legislation. For example, teachers must receive permission from the school district to possess firearms, and local law enforcement departments must work with school employees to train the teachers in firearm safety. We suppose that the reference to the school district means the school board. Reportedly, the new gun law is aimed at school districts that do not have funds to hire trained security personnel. Apparently it has not been decided if the school board will pay for the guns under the classroom materials and supplies fund.

As one would expect, the new South Dakota law is controversial. There always are divided opinions on all gun matters. Are South Dakota schools going to witness "blood baths," and how many teachers in the schools are really capable of handling guns? Teachers will have to be trained to handle guns. Will the hours spent in such in-service training be credited toward their professional development requirements? What about homeschooling? Will both parents be approved to carry guns? What if Mrs. Shakey, home economics teacher, shoots herself in the foot while cooking spaghetti? Will she be able to testify against herself? As a side note, lawsuits for injuries from gun fights might have to be decided by school boards. Will gun duels be allowed? Will school board members be permitted to carry guns? If so, what might be the results of a 4 to 4 split vote by members of the school board? Will this "wild west" gun law permit hanging? These questions, of course, make about as much sense as allowing teachers to possess firearms in the first place.

Case #3—*Goss v. Lopez* (1975), 419 U.S. 56e5, 95 S.Ct 1401, 51, L.Ed.2nd 711. Student Suspension

This was another case testing the school principal's authority to suspend students for conduct violations for up to ten days without a hearing. In a class action filed by the students, they argued that suspensions without the opportunity of due process through a hearing was unconstitutional. The Court tended to agree and stated that the students did have certain liberty and property rights under the due process clause of the Fourteenth Amendment. The Court recommended immediate attention to such cases by giving notice of the charges as soon as possible, and if suspension was to exceed ten days, other student safeguards should be implemented.

Case #4—*Honig v. Doe* (1988), 484 U.S. 305, 108, S. Ct. 592, 98 L.Ed. 2d 686. Expulsion of Disabled Students and the "Stay Put" Provision

The "stay put" provision for disabled children states that during the time a due process case is pending, the child must remain in their current educational placement until the dispute is resolved. In the case of *Honig v. Doe*, two disabled children were suspended for five days for several serious school violations. The case went on over a considerable time period during which time the school was preparing for expulsion proceedings. The students filed a lawsuit arguing that the suspension violated their stay put rights under the Education for All Handicapped Children Act. The South Carolina Supreme Court agreed that the lengthy suspension did result in a change of placement and so it violated the Disabilities Act. The Court set forth several significant statements. For example, the Court held that schools can suspend disabled students (remove them from present programs) for up to ten days when they endanger the safety of others. However, the Court stressed the point that any case in which the student's behavior and his or her disability had to be considered in any attempt to expel the student from school, due process was necessary.

Case #5—*Baker v. Owen*, Corporal Punishment, 96 S. Ct. 210 (1975). Another Corporal Punishment Perspective

The U.S. Supreme Court supported the position that fair, reasonable, and appropriate corporal punishment does not violate the Eighth Amendment. The ruling did establish some interesting ground rules that school principals need to observe. For example, the Court underscored the need to inform students that certain behavior violations may result in corporal punishment. In addition, other punishment measures should be considered and implemented before using corporal punishment, and a second school official must be present when corporal punishment is administered. In cases in which the student's parent requests an explanation of reasons for the punishment, the principal must provide such information and include the name of the school official that was present at the time corporal punishment was administered.

In a related matter, teachers and administrators must be cognizant of the laws concerned with child abuse. They are legally required to report any incidences of child abuse or even suspected child abuse to the proper authorities. Not doing so could lead to personal civil liability and a lawsuit for damages.

Case #6—*Singleton v. Jackson Municipal Separate School District*, 419, F.2d 1211 (56h Cir., 1970). Discrimination in Personnel Practices

Federal laws and court rulings affect virtually every personnel process in which the school principal is involved. In the case of *Singleton v. Jackson Municipal Separate School District*, discrimination in personnel employment practices was asserted. The court's decision underscored the importance of legal practices in all phases of personnel employment practices. Each of the personnel processes of recruitment, protection, development, hiring, place-ment, compensation, evaluation, suspension, tenure, and dismissal must be implemented within the legal laws, statutes, policies, and court rulings of federal, state, and local governing agencies.

Case #7—*Holt v. Shelton*, 341 F. Supp. 821 (M. D. Tenn. 1972). Student Pregnancy

When an expectant mother's physician approves continued attendance in school, pregnant students are permitted to continue in school in all instances. Confirmation of the physician's sanction must be on file with the school.

Pregnant students do not lose their rights and privileges to receive a public education. In addition, they may take part in the school's extracurricu-lar activities unless there is a reason set forth by a physician that the student should not do so.

In relation to such matters as pregnancy or marital or parental status, school district policies set forth other considerations such as the student's responsibility for reporting the existing condition, gaining the necessary in-formation regarding the condition, keeping abreast of the situation in ques-tion, various opportunities for the student to continue her education, liabil-ities during the time of pregnancy, and conditions related to the return of a student to school if prolonged absence is involved.

The foregoing cases are examples of the many court rulings that affect the work of the school principal. In chapters 3 and 4, many other cases involving teachers and students are discussed. In the remaining sections of this chapter, legal implications for the principal's position responsibilities are presented. Emphasis is given to curriculum and the law, safety measures in the class-room, school property, parental relations, classified personnel, school funds, instruction of pupils, and others.

CLASSROOM SAFETY MEASURES

Classroom safety includes a myriad of safety precautions and measures from kindergarten to grade twelve. We thought that an important safety point might be made by considering safety measures in a science classroom, and only one aspect of that safety, safe handling of alcohol in the laboratory. Science teachers potentially are liable for negligence in this regard, but school principals bear the overall responsibility for school safety.

The National Science Teachers Association (NSTA, 2015) set forth a comprehensive list of procedures for handling alcohol in a science lab that might even "surprise" a certified science teacher. For example, one of the NSTA procedures states, "Always practice a laboratory demonstration before using it in the classroom." Second, "Don't work alone in the laboratory." We are not certain just how the teacher is expected to accomplish these procedures, but the Association has fourteen more recommended procedures to accompany them. Four additional procedures are listed here for the purpose of demonstrating possible negligence cases.

1. Ensure that all ignition switches are removed from the area near the alcohol.
   Remember that the vapors of methanol and other alcohols are flammable and denser than air.
2. Keep students away from the demonstration table.
3. Know the location of the A-B-C fire extinguisher, fire blanket, eyewash, and shower. These safety items should be in a location where they can be accessed within ten seconds. Teachers should receive training in the use of all of these items.
4. When using any flammable material in a demonstration, be sure there is a shield between the teacher and the students. The shield only protects the students; the teacher is behind the shield, giving a "false sense of security."

From a responsible point of view, NSTA recommends that teachers, before doing a laboratory demonstration, should ask themselves, "What would a reasonable and prudent person do?" We do take the Association's recommendations as being important and serious. As the Association pointed out, "Each year, accidents involving methanol alcohols happen in K–12 schools and students have been burned and in some cases scarred for life as a result of such accidents" (p. 1).

Without question, schools are legally responsible for maintaining a safe and secure school environment. In addition, elementary schools that house younger care are expected to take special care in providing a safe place for them to learn. The Consumer Product Safety Commission has done a great deal to help establish safe environments for children and youth in schools. Certain items used in the schools have been "recalled" due to their safety hazards. For example, the Consumer Product Safety Improvement Act (CPSIA) of 2008 has direct implications for the use of various supplies used in schools, especially for children twelve years of age or younger.

Reportedly, the Lead Free Toys Act was incorporated into this act. CPSIA bans any toy that a child can put into the mouth or any toy or container that has a certain level of lead such as paint. The product must conform to the safety rules of CPSIA. For example, schoolchildren's books have been included among the numerous products that must be tested according to regulations and certified regarding their testing results, the intended use of the product, for whom the product is intended, and whether the product is appropriate for use by children.

LEGAL HANDLING OF SCHOOL FUNDS BY THE SCHOOL PRINCIPAL

Improper handling of school monies is one of the fastest roads to trouble. In one situation, a student activity fund was adopted and administered by the school superintendent. The fund was supplied by student activities at sports events, school plays, car washing programs, earnings from snack and soft drink machines located within the various schools, student musicals, carnivals, and club events. No public tax monies were placed in the fund. The funds were used for such expenses as band uniforms, purchase of athletic equipment, student field trips, admission charges for school-sponsored student events such as school dances, and paying the expenses incurred for printing school yearbooks. In the Kansas case, the school superintendent used the student activity fund to refurnish his administrative office. Of course, he was fired. From a legal standpoint, school funds may be expended only as set forth by state statutes.

School principals report special concerns with the handling of school funds as well. In fact, approximately one-third of the respondents in the legal survey reported previously viewed this responsibility as having serious legal issues/problems. An additional 50 percent was of the opinion that handling school funds was difficult but less serious. Such responsibilities as handling tax credit donations, student activity funds, and merit performance awards were of special note.

Are funds that are based on activities such as those set forth in the previous paragraph subject to school board control? Court cases have ruled that not only are activity funds under the control of the local school board but are also subject to the very same accounting and auditing procedures established for all other school funds. The rationale underscored by the courts is that student activity funds are derived through the use of school facilities, school maintenance and electricity, custodial services, and school personnel supervision. Transferring student activity fund monies to other school budgets or funds is troublesome. In short, all funds must be used for the purposes that they are intended.

There also are special funds that are established for specific purposes such as equipment, construction, and paying school indebtedness. Transfer of these monies to other funds for other purposes is legally prohibited. In some cases, when the purposes of a special fund have been accomplished and totally funded, if there is a surplus in the fund, state statutes will permit the school board to use these surplus funds for another special fund or to be put back into the school district's general fund.

Basic legal principles for school fund control contend that only the school board has the authority to make purchases for the school district and that school taxes may be used only for the purposes for which they are intended. State statutes regulated strictly the extent to which this authority can be delegated to others within the school district. Accounting and auditing regulations serve to examine, assess, and report on the annual budgeting practices. In some cases, state statutes require school districts to show the amount of money allocated for school purposes, how the money was expended and for what purposes, to whom the money was paid, and if the expenditures complied with the statutes of the state.

Perhaps it is necessary to examine the "controls" that school principals actually have concerning the allocation of school funds. The operational fund of a school district commonly consists of four expenditure categories: employee salaries and benefits, utilities, supplies, and others such as travel and conferences expenses. Approximately 90 percent of the operation fund is allocated for the salaries and related expenses for employee benefits, insurance, and other related expenses. Of the remaining 10 percent of the operation fund, approximately 4 percent is spent on utilities, 3 percent on school supplies, and 3 percent on other activities such as staff development, travel, and conferences.

It is clear that the lion's share of the operation budget is based on fixed charges. A school principal might have something to do with only 3 percent of the operating funds. Nevertheless, the statutes and school policies relating to school funding include specific regulations for expending and accounting for funds regardless of the amount in question. "It is important for the school principal to know the sources of financial resources both available and allocated to the school. First, the source of the funding likely will dictate how the funds can be used. Second, when discussing funding with staff, school groups, parents and other community groups, it is imperative that the principal has a basic knowledge and understanding of school funding sources. Third, such sources provide a knowledge base that can be used when seeking additional resources for the school" (Norton & Kelly, 1997, p. 14).

THE CURRICULUM AND THE LOCAL SCHOOL BOARD

The authority of the local school board relative to the establishment of the curriculum for local schools is well established historically. Although the state has the legal authority to establish courses and standards for academic achievement, local school boards have been left to the discretion of the local school board. Winecoff (2015), field representative for the New Jersey School Boards Association, when asked about the school board's role in curriculum, says, "Quite simply it is to approve what is taught, to monitor the process to ensure that what is being 'taught' is learned; and to support the process by making sure resources needed for learning are available and are being used effectively" (p. 1).

Legally, it is the state's responsibility to prescribe courses that must be taught in the school's curriculum, but local school boards may go beyond the state's requirements. In the case of *Smith v. Consolidated School District No. 2* in Missouri, a student sued a wrestling coach for negligence causing personal injury. The plaintiff argued that the State Department had not required wrestling in a school's curriculum but the school district had made it a required part of the curriculum. Negligence on the part of the wrestling instructor also was an important part of the plaintiff's claims. The plaintiff insisted that the inclusion of wrestling in the curriculum was outside the defendant's authority.

The court ruled otherwise. The court stated that it found no evidence to indicate that wrestling was being taught outside the powers and authority granted the school district by statute. Therefore, school districts do have the authority to extend the curriculum beyond the requirements set forth by state statute. In other cases, such activities as school sports activities have been ruled as proper activities for school districts to offer and support.

Most all state statutes prescribe courses that center on good citizenship. On the other hand, courts have ruled consistently against the teaching of religion, school prayer, and religious prayers at school activities. In addition, nothing is to be taught relative to subversive doctrines (e.g., communism). Topics such as the theory of evolution, religious studies, and sex education have been challenged as appropriate for courses in public schools, but most recent court rulings have approved each of these topics as appropriate for public school education. Such practices as experimenting on live animals are prohibited.

Courses that teach the Constitution are a common requirement in all states, and the majority of states require the teaching of the state constitution. In Arizona, the teaching of civics is generally understood as a requirement. In 2015, the state required the passing of a civics test before any student could graduate from high school. Other state mandates include instructional requirements for teaching such common courses as arithmetic, spelling, reading, and others, such as the effects of alcohol and narcotics, health and safety, physical education, and reading.

From time to time, special emphasis is placed on subject areas that have become a public concern. For example, in the early 1960s, the "poor" health of children and youth became a theme of President John Kennedy, and physical education in schools became a priority. *A Nation at Risk* led to a major emphasis on mathematics and science. Vocational/technical education programs have come to the fore periodically over the years as being special needs for America's technology, business, and workforce welfare.

The selection of textbooks for use in public schools has been left primarily to the local school board. However, the case of *Island Trees School District v. Pico* (1982) holds important implications for book selection for libraries and school classrooms. In this case, however, the school board directed the schools to remove nine books from school libraries. Five students sued the school district with the claim that such removal violated their First Amendment rights of free speech. The Supreme Court of the United States ruled in favor of the students with the opinion that the books were not required reading. In other court cases, courts have ruled that school boards cannot remove books from school library shelves just because they do not like their content. Students have the right to learn, and thus schools cannot control their library bookshelves in a narrow, biased manner.

School boards have considerable authority concerning how schools are to be organized, including graded or nongraded classrooms and a combination of grade levels (e.g., kindergarten through six, seven through nine, ten through twelve, kindergarten through five, six through eight, or nine through twelve), or school boards can allow pupils to skip grades if such a promotion is warranted. Court cases have ruled that the school board has the discretion to determine whether or not a child with the ability can skip a grade. However, the ability to skip a grade does not compel the school board to permit it. Court evidence makes it quite clear that the local school board has the authority to determine school policies and procedures relative to student retention in a grade, student promotion, and student placement. As emphasized throughout the chapter, laws related to curriculum and instruction have been left primarily within the control and jurisdiction of the school board, professionally prepared principals, and certificated teachers.

LIABILITY OF SCHOOL BOARD MEMBERS

When it comes to the topic of liability and local school boards, it is necessary to refer to each state's statutes. It has been established that school boards exercise their authority only as a "body of the whole"; board members have no such authority when acting individually. Since a school district is an extension of state authority, courts in some states have ruled that school districts are not liable for torts committed by its board members, representatives, or employees. When the school board is acting in the performance of exercising a governmental function, some courts have ruled that it is immune from tort liability. However, this issue tends to be somewhat confusing since the record shows that states have passed laws permitting school districts to be sued for reasons of tort liability. Many court cases have been filed concerning such matters as breach of contract, dangerous and defective conditions of school grounds, and misuse of school funds.

It is commonly agreed that school board members are not personally liable for defamation of character, which occurs in the course of discretionary acts within the scope of their authority. When statements are made that tend to "injure" the respect, esteem, or reputation of a person, *defamation* can occur. The term *libel* is used when such statements are in written form. When used verbally, defamation is termed *slander.* When defamation occurs in the course of the discretionary acts of the school board members' authority, board members are most often not held personally liable.

In the early case of *McCormick v. Burt*, the court stated that school board members should not be held liable for errors in judgment. As noted by the court, "In such cases the law seems to be well settled there can be no action maintained against school officers when they act without malice" (1880). However, some fifty-six years later, the Mississippi Supreme Court stated: "It is true that officers are not liable for the honest exercise of discretionary powers confided to them, but when they go outside their powers and commit wrongs under the color of office, there is liability. They are not given immunity from willful wrongs or malicious acts."

INDIVIDUALS WITH DISABILITIES EDUCATION ACT (IDEA) 1990

The 1975 Education for All Handicapped Children Act (EHA) was revolutionary in that it removed discrimination of children with disabilities and opened the door for them to participate in the school's programs and services presently being enjoyed by other students. Preschool and infant-toddler educational provisions were added in 1986. The 1990 Individuals with Disabilities Education Act (IDEA) stated that each child was to be placed in the least restrictive environment (LRE) that allowed for his or her educational progress to continue. Such an environment included that of working in normal classrooms with other children that were not disabled. Disabled students were to be educated as they would have been without the disability.

Disabled students were to have an Individual Educational Plan (IEP) planned by the teacher(s), parents, and the student. Achievement progress was to be measured, monitored, and assessed in order to assure that achievement progress was indeed being realized. It seems important to note that school principals reportedly indicate that their work with special education programs in their schools requires approximately one-third of their work time.

SCHOOL PRINCIPALS AND THE RIGHTS AND RESPONSIBILITIES OF PARENTS

Several court cases have tested the rights of parents to complain about the actions of teachers toward a student. The case of *Segall v. Piazza* is significant in regard to a parent's need to prove that statements set forth by the defense are false. In this case, the parent (Piazza) claimed that the teacher had injured her son by "slamming" his head into his desk, causing his nose to bleed. In the case at hand, Segall sought damages for injury to his reputation and standing in the community. The court ruled that the plaintiff must provide evidence that the acts he or she performed were actuated by expressed malice or actual ill will. That is, the law requires parents and teachers involved in a dispute to communicate their knowledge about the incident, and charges must be proven as true. In this case, the court ruled in favor of the teacher.

As is true with most laws on education, rights of parents differ from state to state. One reference set forth eighteen "potential" rights of parents with children in public schools (Parent Voices, 2015, July 13). The reference is quick to point out the importance of viewing their listing of "parental rights" as conditional and typically reasonable for parents to expect. We have selected ten of the eighteen parental rights to demonstrate what courts are most likely to support.

- Meet with teachers, as well as consult with other professionals interacting with their children at school, including counselors, coaches, administrators, and others.
- Request a change in class or teacher assignment for their child.
- Inspect their child's school records, including academic, counseling, and health information.
- Request a time to visit the school and observe their child's classes.
- Be notified when medical services are being offered to their child.
- Expect and request an educational environment that is emotionally and physically safe for their children.
- Be informed of and have the right to appeal school policies and administrative decisions.
- Receive written notice and the option to opt their child out of surveys that include invasive questions about students' sexual experiences or attrac-

tions, their families' beliefs, morality, religion, political affiliations, or mental and psychological problems of the student or family members.

- Request and arrange a time to examine textbooks, lesson plans, curriculum, and supplemental materials used in their child's classroom.
- Be notified if the school is aware that their child has been bullied or has been accused of bullying.

For many years, concerns on the part of educators centered on the lack of involvement in school matters. The thinking was that if only parents would get to know us they would give us the support that we need to educate their children. In fact, parents and parents' associations did get involved and became knowledgeable of their rights and other facts relative to school procedures and operations. The result has been not only the support of parents but also just how the school officials intend to deliver on the rights of parents. Support has become a two-way street.

It does seem clear that parents cannot interfere with the responsibilities of school officials (*Segall v. Piazza*, 1965). This court case held that parents do have a right to criticize a teacher or an administrator. However, the parent does run the risk of defamation and must be able to prove the charges set forth. Additionally, court rulings appear to support the fact that school boards are free from taking the advice of citizens unless it so chooses. That is, the board of education has a right to be free from interference in the performance of their duties imposed by a state's constitution and legislative statutes.

The *Sullivan v. the New York Times* court case (1964) considered the question of whether a public official could recover damages for a defamatory falsehood relating to his or her official conduct. The court ruled that an official could not recover damages of this nature unless he or she could provide evidence that the statements indeed were false and made with actual malice; that is, it was made with the knowledge that it was false or made with "malice" and not caring whether the statements were true or false. The doctrine of qualified privilege will usually protect teachers and administrators from liability for defamation of character. However, they will become liable for defamation of character if they indiscriminately communicate to others defamatory material concerning either pupils or other school employees (Peterson et al., 1978, p. 283).

PARENTAL DIVORCE/CUSTODIAL POLICIES AND PROCEDURES

Each year a large number of the parents of schoolchildren divorce, posing complex issues of custody and the continuing education of the child. Fagan and Rector (2000) point out that over one million children encounter the divorce of their parents each year. Research and empirical evidence point out that the occurrence of divorce results in devastating physical, emotional, and financial effects on children. Such children do more poorly in academic performance, are increasingly subjects of abuse, exhibit more health and behavioral problems, are more involved in drug abuse, and have a higher rate of suicide. In addition, children of divorced parents are far more likely to be retained in a school grade and are likely subjects for dropping out of school altogether.

The responsibilities of school principals and other professional educators depend largely on the rulings of divorce courts and the procedures set forth in the school district's policies related to students with divorced or separated parents. The School District of Philadelphia sets forth such procedures in its policy titled Rights of the Custodial and Non-Custodial Parents. The school district's policy is presented in part only in the following section. The entry is an example of one school district and should not be viewed as the appropriate legal policy for all school districts.

RIGHTS OF CUSTODIAL AND NON-CUSTODIAL PARENTS

I. Registration/School Records

    a. When a parent or legal guardian notifies the school that the student is to be called by a family name recorded on the birth certificate, the student may be called by the requested name.

    b. However, on all official school records, the names appearing on the birth certificate must be recorded.

    c. Only on presentation of a Court Order indicating a change of the student's name may official school records be changed.

    d. When an individual claims to be a parent or legal guardian, and no reference to that person appears in existing school records, the school is to request the production of a certified birth certificate or court order verifying the legal relationship.

    e. When school personnel are not acquainted with a person appearing before them as being a parent or legal guardian, proper identification must be presented and recorded before the student, or information concerning the student, is released.

II. Custodial Parent

For the purposes of this policy, the parent with custody of a student during the school week, whether by Court Order, written agreement, or actual circumstances, is the custodial parent.

III. Custodial Court and Protective Orders

a. When it is learned that a student's parents are divorced or separated, the principal shall request that the custodial parent provide the school with a copy of the latest Court Order (custody and/or protective) and/or custody agreement.

IV. Special Education Proceedings

Unless a court order terminates parental rights or specifically deprives a parent of the right to participate in educational decisions, either parent may initiate the hearing process in special education matters. When a non-custodial parent has requested that he/she be informed of all planning conferences and/or IEPS, such must be provided.

V. Visitation or Release of Students

1. Schools should not be the location of visits between students and parents (custodial or noncustodial).
2. A student is not to be released to a noncustodial parent unless such release is authorized by a current Court Order, or is approved by the custodial parent, in a verified written communication.
3. If neither a Court Order nor formal custody arrangements for the student have been established, the principal is to defer to the parent with whom the student resides.
4. If the release of a student is approved, all procedures set forth in printed procedures are to be followed.
5. When there is reason to believe that a disagreement between parents may cause a physical confrontation over the physical custody of a student, the principal may call the police, or if time allows, seek advice from the office of General Counsel.
6. At no time while establishing the identity of a parent, or of ascertaining the rights of divorced or separated parents, are students to be brought into the view or contact with the alleged parent.

A point to remember is that education and divorce laws vary from state to state, so it is of paramount importance for school personnel to be cognizant of the laws in their state and preferably have an informed attorney in the state serve as the source for legal advice. Divorce does not limit education rights, but the legal documents that set forth the responsibilities and relationships of parents and school personnel loom significant in deciding the various procedures for the important decisions that school principals and other school personnel must determine.

THE SCHOOL PRINCIPAL AND CLASSIFIED PERSONNEL

As American citizens, classified/support personnel enjoy all of the rights of any citizen under the U.S. Constitution. The literature reports that the rights of classified personnel are much the same as the rights of other school personnel, with certain exceptions. For example, one court case ruled that a school secretary had no expectations of continued employment and therefore had no rights to a due process hearing upon being terminated. In a different termination case, the court ruled that a due process was appropriate if it involved the potential for future employment.

Approximately 60 percent of the school principals participating in the legal survey viewed classified personnel issues/problems as being serious or difficult but less serious. The point in question here is that of attempting to distinguish between constitutional and statutory requirements and standards. In the court case of *Crampton v. Harmon* (1975), Crampton was a secretary who had been discharged by the school board. As stated by the court, "When considering whether a hearing is required as part of the governmental decision-making process, and, if so, the exact nature of the hearing, it is important to distinguish between constitutional and statutory requirements . . . constitutional authorities set minimum standards that must sometimes be complied with in the decision-making process. However, the Oregon legislature can, and has, enacted statutes that require hearing in situations where the constitution does not. And the legislature can establish hearing procedures that go beyond the constitutional minimums" (p. 1).

In a case of a public city employee (*Williams v. Civil Service Commission*, 1973), Williams was terminated from his position of dogcatcher and was not granted a hearing. Williams was not granted a hearing on the basis of the city ordinance that stated that a temporary employee could be terminated at any time at the discretion of the appointing authority, and a temporary employee who has been terminated shall have no right of appeal to the Civil Service Commission. The appeals court reversed the termination decision in favor of the plaintiff, Williams.

Most state laws require school districts to get background checks for all new employees, including classified personnel. The question often arises as to whether a nonemployee who is working with a student on campus can be required to obtain a background check and/or take his or her fingerprints. It appears that a school board could indeed require a nonemployee such as an intern or social worker to have a background check if the school district's policies were in accordance with state statutes and the regulations set forth by the state Board of Education. Such cautions are in line with a school district's objectives of ensuring a safe and secure learning environment for students and staff throughout the school district.

THE SCHOOL PRINCIPAL AS HUMAN RESOURCES LEADER

Norton (2015) points out that the processes of the human resources function increasingly are being delegated to the local school principal. Licensure for the principal's position commonly includes only one course on the subject of personnel administration. As Smith (1998) noted, "The principal's ability to provide effective leadership to the human resources function of the school, will, in large measure, determine the effectiveness of the school and the teachers" (p. 6). Recall the primary processes of the human resources function: recruitment, selection, orientation, placement, development, evaluation, and retention. Each of these processes carries with it implications for legal responsibilities and liabilities on the part of the school principal.

In the following section, we discuss the human resources function in relation to the legal implications of each process. As previously noted, we discuss the legal responsibilities of the school principal in relation to the work of schoolteachers and school students in detail in chapters 3 and 4. The personnel section is introduced by the following true or false quiz. Give your answer to each of the questions, and then check the correct answers at the end of the quiz.

LEGAL QUESTIONS CONCERNING THE HUMAN RESOURCES PROCESSES

1. Statutory rights of employees are protected by the school board policies set forth by respective school boards. ____T or ____F
2. Contractual rights of employees are based on state statutes. ____T or ____F
3. Courts have held that academic freedom is fundamental to our democratic society. ____T or ____F
4. Title VII of the Civil Rights Act of 1964 prohibits employment discrimination based on race, color, religion, sex, and national origin. ____T or ____F
5. Title VII of the Civil Rights Act of 1964 prohibits sexual harassment of students. ____T or ____F
6. Quid pro quo harassment occurs when a female or male applicant for a school position suggests they will provide sexual favors if they are hired for the position in question. ____T or ____F
7. Which of the entries below commonly are used for the dismissal of school employees by most states?

    a. Incompetence
    b. Willful neglect of duty
    c. Immorality

   d. Misconduct

   e. Insubordination

8. State statutes in each of the fifty states give the school superintendent the legal authority to terminate teachers from school positions. ____T or ____F

9. The 1988 Federal Drug-Free Workplace Act requires the firing or demotion of any school principal whenever a student or licensed employee is found guilty of using drugs on campus or off campus by police or school security officers ____T or ____F

10. A new teacher is hired and the contract states that she is hired to teach grade 1. When the teacher arrives on the job, she learns that she has been assigned grade 5. The teacher has a legal right to refuse the new teaching assignment. ____T or ____F

11. The Age Discrimination Act of 1967 recognizes the "probability of stress" on teachers with substantial service. The Act then states that individuals who are forty years of age or older should not be expected to be protected from "job loss" due to such events as reduction in force or school district reorganization. ____T or ____F

12. The Pregnancy Act of 1978 provides some protection for female workers who are pregnant, but excessive use of sick leave or "resting during preparation periods" that are designed for lesson planning are reasons for reevaluating the teacher's continuation on the job. ____T or ____F

13. The Rehabilitation Act of 1973 was amended in 1992 so that individuals who are currently engaging in the illegal use of drugs could be included in the provision of the Act. ____T or ____F

14. If you saw the code GABC on a memorandum sent to you by the central office of the school district, you would know immediately that the memo topic was that of a:

   a. Curriculum matter

   b. Student personnel matter

   c. Budget matter

   d. Personnel matter

15. The term *classified personnel* refers to:

   a. Those persons in the school district that have reached tenure

   b. Those persons in the school district that hold specific job titles

   c. Those persons in the school district that are noncertificated

   d. Those persons in the school district that have passed the requirement or are hired to teach in one subject area only or in one elementary grade level only (e.g., science, industrial arts, primary grades, intermediate grades)

16. Joint legal custody of a child means that both parents keep the right to make important decisions about their children's education, health care, and religious training. _____T or _____F

Answers to the Legal Quiz with Comments

1. Question #1, statutory rights of employees are protected by the school board policies set forth by respective school boards, is false. Such rights are determined by the legislatures of each state and approved by them. School board policies may provide for teacher rights, but they cannot conflict with the rights set forth in legislative statutes. In addition, school boards may extend the rights set forth in state statutes just as long as they do not exceed the school board's authority or be contrary to federal or state law. School boards may set higher standards than required in such areas as physical and health qualifications, experience, advanced degrees, and the number of credit hours required for teaching a subject.

2. Question #2, contractual rights of employees are set forth by state statutes, is false. Contact law provides the basis for contractual procedures. When employees sign a teaching contract, it commonly is assumed that they also have "endorsed" the policies and regulations set forth by the school board as well.

3. Question #3, courts have ruled that academic freedom is fundamental to our society, is true. Courts have consistently supported free speech in the classroom as long as it is directly related to the educational theme of the instructional lesson. The use of vulgarity, for example, has been ruled OK when it is used for the purposes of education. Although the teaching of religion in public schools is strictly prohibited, teaching the history of religions has been viewed as appropriate. In a different situation, speech by a teacher that is defamatory against the school principal is not illegal if proof can be provided that the remarks were indeed true and not falsely made in malice. In chapter 3, the case of *Pickering v. Board of Education* (1968) gives additional insight into the matter of teacher free speech.

4. Question #4, Title VII of the Civil Rights Act prohibits employment discrimination based on race, color, religion, sex, or national origin, is true. These rights loom important in the personnel function and its processes of recruiting, hiring, promotion, benefits, and dismissal.

5. Question #5, Title VII of the Civil Rights Act prohibits sexual harassment of students, is false. Title VII considers sexual harassment in the workplace. Sexual harassment of students is included in Title IX in amendments set forth in 1972.

6. Question #6, quid pro quo harassment occurs when a female or male applicant for a school position suggests that they will provide sexual favors if they are hired for the position, is false. Just reverse the situation. When a potential employer suggests to a candidate that the position would more than likely be available to them if they would perform sexual favors, the behavior is indeed quid pro quo harassment.

7. Question #7, which of the entries below are commonly used for the dismissal of employees by most states? The five listings, a, b, c, d, and e, reportedly are the most common factors in employee dismissal cases. Incompetence leads the listing. The term *incompetence* was defined by the court in one case as "lack of ability or fitness to discharge the required duty" (*Horosko v. Mount Pleasant PL'T TWP.*, S. Dist, 1939). Incompetency has been closely associated with the term *inefficiency.* As Nolte (1973) points out, both terms reveal a lack of requisite ability. In addition, incompetency can extend into other areas of a teacher's life.

   The *Horosko v. Mount Pleasant School District* case, although most interesting, was originally ruled in favor of the school board. Horosko was terminated due to the fact that her behavior was contrary to the morals of the community and thus, as claimed, was a bad example to the youth in the school. In brief, the teacher worked as bartender in her husband's restaurant and served beer to customers in front of her students, drank beer occasionally, and played with the restaurant's pinball machines and rolled dice in the restaurant's games.

   The term *incompetency* was studied in depth by the courts involved in the determination of the case. The definition of the term became a decision point of the case itself. Ultimately, the Supreme Court of the state of Pennsylvania reversed the order of the Superior Court that had ruled in favor of the teacher. The teacher's dismissal for incompetency was upheld. In order to gain more insight into the importance and complexity of this case, the reader should study the case in its entirety. As the State Supreme Court noted, "Incompetency does not mean merely the ability to teach the Three R's, it goes further than that. We therefore conclude that it would be 'just' to affirm the action of the board in dismissing the teacher."

8. Question #8, state statutes in each of the fifty states give the school superintendent the legal authority to terminate teachers from school positions, is false. Although we are well aware of the fact that the large majority of states rule that only the local school board can legally hire or terminate professional teacher personnel, we believe that the state of Connecticut permits the school superintendent to hire teachers. There appears to be some evidence that the school superintendent in

Portland, Maine, has the authority to hire professional teachers as well.

9. Question #9, the 1988 Federal Drug-Free Workplace Act requires the firing or demotion of any school principal whenever a student or licensed employee is found guilty of using drugs on campus or off campus by police or local security officers, is false. In substance abuse cases involving teachers or students, the court rulings have centered on the question, "To what extent did the behavior of the person interrupt or interfere with the educational program of the school?" It seems likely that the courts would not uphold the dismissal of a teacher who was stopped in traffic and the police found marijuana in the car. Unless evidence was found that the situation rendered the teacher unfit for teaching, termination of the teacher would most likely not be upheld. Of course, the Federal Drug-Free Workplace Act has no such requirement. The Act does require school districts that receive $25,000 or more in federal funds to adopt a drug-free workplace and a drug-free environment policy and to disseminate it among all school employees.

10. Question #10, a new teacher is hired and her contract states that she is to teach grade 1. When the teacher arrives on the job, she learns that she has been assigned grade 5. The teacher has a right to refuse the new teaching assignment, is true. A teaching contract has the same provisions as any other legal contract. If the teacher's contract states that the teacher will be assigned to teach grade 1, unless the teacher agrees to do so, she cannot be required to teach another grade.

11. Question #11, the Age Discrimination Act of 1967 recognizes the "probability of stress" of teachers with substantial service. The Act then states that teachers who are forty years of age or older should not be expected to be protected from "job loss" due to such events as reduction in force or school district reorganization, is false. The Act strictly prohibits any discrimination of persons forty years of age or older for any reason whatsoever. These individuals are to be treated as any other school employee would be treated under the conditions being encountered by the school district.

12. Question #12, the Pregnancy Act of 1978 provides some protection for female workers who are pregnant, but excessive use of sick leave or "resting during class preparation periods" that are designed for lesson planning are reasons for reevaluating the teacher's continuation on the job, is false.

13. Question #13, the Rehabilitation Act of 1973 was amended in 1992 so that individuals who are currently engaging in the illegal use of drugs could be included in the provisions of the Act, is false. The Act

was amended in 1992 so as to *exclude* individuals who are currently engaging in the illegal use of drugs.

14. Question #14, if you saw the code GBAC on a memorandum sent to you by the central office of the school district, you would know immediately that the topic of the memo was that of (d), a Personnel matter. The letter "G" in the NEPN/NSBA policy codification system represents the personnel section for school policies. That is, "G" represents the section or series, "B" represents the second section, "A" represents the first division, and "C" represents the third subdivision in the policy listing.

15. Question #15, the term *classified personnel* refers to (c) those persons in the school district that are noncertificated.

16. Question #16, joint legal custody of a child means that both parents have a right to make important decision about their children's education, health care, and religious training, is true. Unless the court has ruled otherwise, joint custody gives both parents the right to participant in a handicapped child's IEP decisions, be given notice of IEP team meeting times and rights to attend, receive the child's progress reports, and to exercise their own personal rights under the Constitution.

In the final sections of chapter 2, we discuss a variety of legal cases and responsibilities of school principals. For example, the specific types of liability for school principals, communication responsibilities, pupil records, special education laws, and the admission and attendance of pupils are discussed, and the chapter closes with a summary of Civil Rights Acts that are not detailed in other chapters of the book.

THE SCHOOL PRINCIPAL AND RELEASE OF A PUPIL'S EDUCATIONAL RECORDS

The U.S. Department of Education has set forth important information that gives parents certain rights regarding the access to their child's school records. The Family Educational Rights Act and Privacy Act (FERPA) gives parents protection regarding the use of a pupil's school records (e.g., report cards, disciplinary records, family information, transcripts, etc.). Parents now have the right to gain access to their child's school records and to refuse to release the records to persons other than themselves. The primary purpose of such protection, of course, is that of privacy. Although parents requesting to review their child's records must receive approval within forty-five days, in some cases state laws require such access sooner than the forty-five-day requirement. In any case, the school principal cannot allow others to review a child's records without the parents' permission. The principal is not required to send copies of the school records to parents except in limited circumstances (U.S. Department of Education, July 2015).

When a student reaches age eighteen, all rights concerning student records is placed in the hands of the individual student. At this point, even the parents must obtain permission from their child to review educational records. There are certain exceptions concerning the review of student records. For example, FERPA allows certain leeway for releasing information such as *directory information* related to student directories, degrees and honors, participation in school activities, and others that are viewed as harmless and/or not an invasion of privacy.

STUDENT SCHOOL ADMISSION AND ATTENDANCE

The courts have left the age requirements for school admission and attendance much to the discretion of the states and local school boards. In doing so, there are differences among the states relative to the ages specified for school attendance. Whenever school boards are acting with reason and within the laws of the state, courts are reluctant to review decisions relative to these matters. In this same manner, courts will not interfere with the determination of school boundary lines for student attendance (*McEwan v. Broad*, 91 N.Y. S.2nd 565 [1949]). Court cases in Iowa and Ohio have also confirmed the theory that school boards are in the best position to establish school boundaries and to determine the schools that students will attend.

School boards have the authority to set health and "cleanliness" standards for student attendance. For example, courts have supported the power of school boards to exclude pupils that do not meet health requirements or have not been immunized as required. The requirement of immunization programs for students has been contested in at least eleven states and ruled as "approved" in each case. Courts have supported the exclusion of students for having head lice and trachoma (a chronic contagious mucous membrane), and also have supported the authority of school boards to adopt appropriate health regulations for the benefit of the students, staff, and members of the citizenry. Of course, there have been numerous court cases testing the authority of school boards to require vaccinations. The practice continues to be supported, including vaccinations for students in private schools.

Age requirements for school attendance differ among the states as well. Although it is common for states to provide education for students from ages six to twenty-one, legislative support commonly has been given to school boards to offer prekindergarten, kindergarten, and post–high school programs, stating that there is nothing in the constitution prohibiting better education for such purposes as vocational education and educational programs for adults.

THE RIGHT TO OPT OUT OF STUDENT TESTING

Mandated student testing remains a primary topic of contention in most every state nationally. There is no question that student testing is one of the leading issues and problems facing school principals today. Although state testing requirements tend to differ among the many states, a key question being asked is "Do parents have a legal right to opt out of testing of their children?" A recent Arizona attorney general's opinion is that the answer to the question is no; parents do not have a legal right to withdraw their children from state-mandated assessments in public schools (*The Arizona Republic*, October 12, 2015, p. 6A).

Of course, an attorney general's opinion is just that, a probable opinion rather than a ruling as would be set forth by a court of law. In setting forth the foregoing opinion, the attorney general underscored the rationale that the state legislature did intend to include the right to opt out of statewide assessments and the state legislature has limited the authority of parents to "customize" that education.

EDUCATIONAL LAW AS RELATED TO SPECIAL EDUCATION PROGRAMS IN PUBLIC SCHOOLS

"Before the enactment of the Education for All Handicapped Children Act (EAHCA) in 1975, only 20 percent of children with disabilities were being educated by public schools in the United States. In 1975, some states still had laws that excluded children with certain disabilities from attending public school" (Norton, Kelly, & Battle, 2012, p. 96). In addition, The National Council on Disability reported that before the Act was passed, more than one million children in America had no access to an education in public schools.

Presently, school programs include some twenty-two different student disabilities in their special education programs from attention deficit disorder to speech and language impairments, to autism, to mental retardation, to dyslexia, to bipolar disorder, and others. Student special services encompass approximately twelve student special services from psychological services to occupational therapy to evaluation and referral services to rehabilitation counseling to homeschooling to social work services and others. In recent years, statutory enactments and court rulings have greatly extended the opportunity for disabled students to enjoy the full complex of programs and activities that public schools can provide.

It is clear, however, that the level of support for special needs students must be commensurate with the level of support of other educational and governmental activities but should not exceed that level. That is, the financing of a near-ideal situation for one particular segment of society should not be injurious to other segments of society (Peterson et al., 1978).

Three acts set forth the large majority of the responsibilities of schools and school principals for students with special needs. Section 504 of the Rehabilitation Act of 1973 guaranteed the participation of all school-age individuals with disabilities to be able to gain the benefits of any public school program receiving federal financing. Such participation includes those programs and activities that take place outside the regular school program hours (e.g., school clubs, extracurricular activities, athletics, school plays, and others).

The Education for All Handicapped Children Act of 1975 (EHA) served to reinforce the participation of disabled students in the educational programs and services of the public school by removing discrimination against children with disabilities. In 1986, the EHA was amended to include infant-toddler program provisions, and in 1990 the Act was renamed the Individuals with Disabilities Education Act (IDEA). At the same time, the Act added the "least restrictive environment" (LRE) to the Act that stated the student was to be educated in a program in the least restrictive environment that assured learning success. In this sense, the student had to be placed in a program whereby academic progress was assured for the student.

Each disabled student was required to have and implement an Individual Educational Plan (IEP) that was best suited to his or her special needs and interests. The student, parents, teachers, and other appropriate officials and individuals were to work out the IEP and sign off on its approval. The Act carries strong implications for the school principal in planning, implementing, monitoring, and assessing the academic improvement of each disabled student in the school.

KEY IDEAS AND RECOMMENDATIONS SET FORTH IN CHAPTER 2

- *Court Rulings and Governmental Statutes*: Virtually all of the state and federal court rulings hold implications for the work responsibilities of the school principal. Even when a court case involves the school district's Board of Education, the ruling outcome(s) commonly hold new implications for the principal's office.
- *Court Rulings and Governmental Statutes Are Always Evolving*: Chapter 2 underscored the point that court decisions are ruled, appealed, mandated, reviewed, and set aside in an ever-changing society. School principals are

not expected to be legal attorneys; however, their position responsibilities make it necessary for them to keep abreast of legal rulings and state statutes that invariably will come to rest in their school office. Possessing knowledge of historical court rulings and state statutes serves the positive purpose of being aware of common legal problem areas and understanding the need for using caution and reasonableness in administrative decisions.

- *Some Laws Rise to the Front of the Principal's Responsibilities*: Without question, the court cases and state statutes must be given priority attention. Student suspension, corporal punishment, student welfare and safety, funding controls, teacher dismissal, students with disabilities, and classified personnel are among those matters that consistently are being contested in the courts. Keeping abreast of "happenings" in these areas of legal contention looms important for school principals.
- *Administration of School Funds*: It is clear that the school principal's understanding and implementation of school budgeting and auditing must be given high priority. All school funds of any kind are viewed as school district funds and must only be expended for purposes for which they are intended.
- *Curriculum and School Law*: It is clear that state legislatures have the authority to establish and control what is taught in the public school. State legislatures and state Boards of Education have determined what must be taught and what cannot be taught in public school programs. However, state legislatures have delegated curriculum matters to local school boards and are reluctant to interfere with curricular decisions unless state statutes or regulations have been violated. In the case of states requiring certain curricula, state offices have not limited such offerings to only those that are required. That is, local school districts are not prohibited from offering more courses that lead to an improved educational program for students.
- *School Board Liability*: State statutes determine the liability of school boards and school board members for torts and other forms of negligence and incompetence. For the most part, school board members are considered immune from the negligence and injuries caused by the employees of the school district. Nevertheless, negligence and incompetence on the part of school employees can result in personal tort liability. Having a good knowledge and understanding of one's legal world will go far in obviating certain problems that are common in the daily activities of school leaders.
- *Classified Personnel*: The rights of classified personnel are the same as any other school employee with some exceptions. Exceptions come in the way of tenure property rights and any guarantee of continuous employment. All of the rights enjoyed by citizens of the United States under the First Amendment are enjoyed by classified personnel of the school district.

- *The Legal Responsibilities of the School Principal as Human Resources Leader*: Many of the human resources processes that historically have been administered by the central school district office are increasingly being delegated to the local school level. The legal implications of recruiting, selecting, assigning, developing, evaluating, terminating, and compensating classified personnel have legal implications. Unfortunately, the large majority of preparation programs for school administrators has one three-hour-credit course in personnel administration. The need for school principals to become knowledgeable and skilled in the law of school personnel is of paramount importance.

- *Pupil Admission and Attendance*: Pupil admission procedures and attendance requirements have largely been delegated to local school boards. As long as state statutes are observed in deciding such matters as the ages of pupils for education in the school district, decisions regarding the school that a student will attend, and student absenteeism, they are left to the discretion of local school boards.

- *Divorce and Parental Custody*: Principals increasingly are being confronted with issues related to divorce and parental custody of their children. Best advice tends to center on the need for school principals to be knowledgeable of their state's legislative and court rules that condition this issue. Knowledge of the present state legislation and court rulings for each case of child custody and following the specific orders will serve the school principal well.

DISCUSSION QUESTIONS

1. Assume that you have just been assigned a new position as a school principal. Be proactive and identify several priority legal matters that you would attend. For example, what might be done relative to checking on a secure and safe school environment?

2. As school principal, your industrial arts teacher reports that a student started a fight with another student and ended up breaking through a glass door in the classroom. The teacher remarks, "What that kid needs is a few swats with a rubber hose." What is your reaction to this situation?

3. You send a memo to your teaching faculty that each member is to stand by the door outside the classroom between classes and supervise student behavior in the hallways. At a meeting of the staff after school, one teacher stands and comments, "We are here to teach our subjects. Now we are asked to police the school campus and student behavior in the hallways. I, for one, refuse to comply with these kinds of orders.

My contract does not include serving as a security officer." As principal, how do you respond?

4. Your elementary school faculty members have been complaining about having to "teach" students with disabilities in the regular classroom with other students. They say that the amount of time needed to instruct these students detracts from the time they can spend with other students. How might you address this issue?

5. Assume that you are a member of your state's Supreme Court. The matter of a free and effective education comes before the court in the case of *Parents v. State Legislative* on the matter of educational funding. Parental educational fees for school supplies, participation in certain courses, extracurricular activities, laboratory fees, books and materials, and other school expenses increasingly have been placed on the shoulders of parents. Parents argue that the student's right to a free and effective education has been violated. Take a position on this matter and set forth your ruling with appropriate legal support.

CASE STUDIES

Case Study #2.1 The Case of Where the Money Goes

You have been transferred from the position of assistant school principal to a principal's position in a high school in the same school district. You have an opportunity to visit the school toward the close of the school year just before you are to take over the reins at the new high school. One of the matters that you examine is that of the school's budget and its accounting procedures. You note that the operating fund has been used to the fullest extent, but there is no mention of other monies that might be obtained from a number of sources such as student activities, sports events, admission fees, donations, and rental fees. These monies are handled by several individual faculty personnel and not accounted in any way in the school funding reports. For example, the director of athletics expends independently the income from sports events. Another fund is handled by the Girls Athletic Association from income from sales of snacks, candy, and beverages at school sports events and other student activities. An annual "donation" from the parent-teacher association for student activities is handled by the school principal, and in one instance it was used to remodel the faculty lounge.

Give thought to the court rulings and other information set forth in chapter 2 relative to the administration of school finance. What actions will be needed on your part to correct the present funding procedures of the school that you will be leading next fall?

Case Study #2.2 We Want a Special Course on the Abuses of Alcohol and Substance Abuse

A representative group of members from a community church group asks for an appointment with you as principal to discuss a curriculum matter. You agree to meet with them. At the meeting, members of the church group hand you a petition insisting on a course on the abuses of alcohol and illegal substances. They state that a deacon in their church is a former teacher licensed to teach social studies and would be an excellent person to teach and/or plan the course. The group also informs you that they have checked with the state statutes and they do not prohibit the teaching of such an important subject.

Since the church is in your school district, the group insists that you take the matter to the school board. As voters in the school district, they infer that they have the right to recommend subjects for the curriculum.

Review the section in chapter 2 on the legal rulings in relation to school curriculum and determine how you will respond to the church group's requests. Will you assume a proactive role in this matter, or just refer the request to the school board?

REFERENCES

Fagan, P. F., & Rector, R. (2000). *The effects of divorce on America.* http://www.heritage.org/research/reports/2000/06/the-effects-of-divorce-on-america.

National Science Teachers Association. (2015). Books and resources: Safe handling of alcohol in the laboratory. Arlington, VA: Author.

Nolte, M. C. (1973). *Duties and liabilities of school administrators.* West Nyack, NY: Parker Publishing Company, Inc.

Norton, M. S. (2008). *Human resources administration for educational leaders.* Thousand Oaks, CA: SAGE.

Norton, M. S., Kelly, L. K., & Battle, A. R. (2012). *The principal as student advocate: Doing what's best for all students.* Larchmont, NY: Eye on Education.

Parent Voices. (2015, July 13). *Parents' rights.* California Care Resource and Referral Network. San Francisco, CA: Author.

Peterson, L. J., Rossmiller, R. A., & Volz, M. M. (1978). *The law and public school operation.* New York: Harper & Row Publishers, Inc.

School District of Philadelphia. (2015, August 8). *Policy and procedures: Rights of the custodial and non-custodial parents.*

United States Department of Education. (2007, October). *Parents' guide to the family educational rights and privacy act: Rights regarding children's education records.* http://www2.ed.gov/policy/gen/guid/fpco/brochures/parents.html.

Winecoff, K. (2012, November/December). The board's role in curriculum: Board members have a critical function in this area. *School Leader, 43,* 2.

Chapter Three

Legal Rights and Liabilities Concerning Teacher Personnel

Primary chapter goal: To discuss the legal rights, protections, and liabilities of teacher personnel in their positions in public schools.

> Teachers and school staff including food services, maintenance and operations, office and clerical, paraeducators, special services and administration enjoy a number of rights pertaining to their employment, including recognition of certain freedoms, prohibition against certain forms of discrimination, and significant protections against dismissal from their position. These rights are derived from state and federal constitutional provisions, state and federal statutes and federal regulations.
> —Steven E. Glink, Teacher and School Staff Rights, June 24, 2015

It is clear that professional personnel working in America's public schools enjoy the same rights as all other citizens. Nevertheless, court rulings and state statutes are prominent relative to both the rights and the liabilities of school personnel. It would be far beyond the scope of this chapter to attempt to include the entire variety of rulings and legal statutes that contend with the legal world of administrators and teachers. Discussions of teachers' rights are inextricably tied to relationships with the school principal, students, and parents. We have selected several major areas of administrator and staff rights and liabilities to discuss.

Chapter 2 focused on the legal rights and liabilities of school principals. The topics of general teacher rights, administrator authority, tenure provisions, teacher discrimination, teacher suspension, teacher liabilities, teacher/student relations, and teacher dismissal are among the major topics discussed in chapter 3.

We begin chapter 3 by asking you to take time to respond to the pre-quiz on the topics at hand. In each case, check true or false for each question posed. Do not simply guess the answer; rather, just skip that question and move to the next question.

PRE-QUIZ ON ADMINISTRATOR/TEACHER PERSONNEL

1. Courts have generally held that teaching certificates are contracts and should be considered as such in practice. T_____ or F_____
2. Teacher and administrative tenure guarantees indefinite employment. T_____ or F_____
3. The general law of contracts relative to agreements between one public party and another in the business field does not apply to teacher contracts since such contracts are under the jurisdiction of an elected school board. T_____ or F_____
4. The Fourteenth Amendment of the U.S. Constitution does not protect teachers while in public schools since the constitution does not include the topic of education in its content. T_____ or F_____
5. In 1967 the Age Discrimination Act was passed prohibiting discrimination against workers over age forty. However, courts have since ruled that the age discrimination law does not apply to teacher personnel since age is "indeed a factor" when working with younger children and youth. T_____ or F_____
6. Teachers or administrators can be fired for "unprofessional behavior," such as being critical of school boards, even though the statements have no effect on school operations or objectives. T_____ or F_____
7. A school principal expelled a handicapped student for violating a published school rule. The school principal followed exactly the same procedures for the student as would be done for any normal student. If contended, the school principal's procedures would be supported. T_____ or F_____
8. A teacher sent an email to her school principal stating that she had problems with the principal's recent "mandate" concerning student retention in a grade. The teacher noted that the decision was contrary to published research and would do more "damage" than good for students. The principal submitted a report to the school superintendent of subordination on the part of the teacher. A hearing on the matter would lead to the teacher's probable dismissal. T_____ or F_____
9. A teacher plans a field trip for his science class. In order to participate, each student is required to have his or her parents/guardians sign a permission slip for the student to attend. In such cases, the teacher

bears no legal responsibility for any injuries that a student might endure during the trip. T_____ or F_____

10. A school principal is attending a school board meeting generally viewed as being required by all local school administrators. The school board is having the third reading of a proposed policy on the topic of student homework. The policy requires such procedures as the time required for homework assignments, signatures by parents that the homework time is accurate, and verification that the homework was indeed the work of the student. The school board chair, who favored the policy, asked for questions or comments from those in attendance. Principal Rodriquez of the Whittier Middle School stands and says, "I respectfully recommend that further study be given this matter before the board's final vote is taken. As a middle school principal, I have several reservations about the wisdom of the proposed homework policy. For example, the policy does not appear to differentiate requirements between schoolchildren at the various school levels. In addition, the requirements of the policy present several problems for its administration."

The board chair indicated that the principal's remarks were a bit late and now it was time to vote. The board vote was 4 to 3 against the policy. After the fact, the school board chair called the school superintendent and expressed the opinion that the school principal had demonstrated insubordination and this matter should be followed up appropriately. In view of the facts presented, the board chair is indeed correct regarding the improper behavior of the school principal. T_____ or F_____

11. Court cases have held that a school district can restrict teachers' classroom speech to curriculum-related topics only. T_____ or F_____

Answers to the Pre-Quiz

In view of the facts presented in each of the foregoing questions, the answers are: question 1 true; question 2 false; question 3 false; question 4 false; question 5 false; question 6 false; question 7 false; question 8 false; question 9 false; question 10 false; and question 11 true. Chapter 3 will give due attention to the pre-quiz questions along with other court rulings and state statues that focus on administrator and teacher legal rights and liabilities. At the outset, however, we discuss several relevant court cases that have greatly influenced administrator and teacher practices.

RELATED COURT CASES

Chapter 3 reviews several court cases related to the questions in the foregoing quiz. For example, the case of *Garcetti v. Ceballos* (2006) answers question 11. In this case, a high school teacher spoke out in her classroom about
the mold in the classroom and her related health problems. The teacher sued
the school district on the basis that her First Amendment rights had been
violated. The court ruled that a school district can restrict a teacher's speech
in the classroom. That is, only topics related to the curriculum can be discussed. In short, a schoolteacher's speech in the classroom is considered
"job-duty speech" and is not protected by the First Amendment. A violation
of this ruling can result in discipline or even discharge.

The Pennsylvania State Education Association (2015, July 31) pointed
out the teachers should avoid taking political stances in the classroom. This
warning followed a situation when a teacher was asked if she ever participated in a political demonstration. She answered that she had honked her car
horn on one occasion when she passed an antiwar demonstration during
nonworking hours. Demonstrators were holding signs that read, "Honk for
Peace." Parents called the school to complain. The teacher's contract was not
renewed, and she filed a lawsuit claiming that her free speech rights had been
violated. The court upheld the school district's decision not to renew the
teacher's contract. Other important court cases regarding teacher rights and
liabilities are cited in the following section.

Case #1—*Pickering v. Board of Education*, 391 U.S. 563, 88S. Ct. 1731 (1968). Teacher's Criticism of School Board and Superintendent

A high school teacher sent a letter to the editor of the local newspaper
criticizing the actions of the school board and school superintendent regarding their handling of school funding. The handling of a school bond issue and
distribution of funds for educational programs and athletics were also contended. The teacher submitted that the school superintendent had attempted
to repress views that opposed the project. The school board scheduled a
hearing that resulted in charging the teacher of defaming the board though
false statements. The teacher was fired.

An Illinois Court sided with the school board. However, the case ultimately went to the U.S. Supreme Court, and the Court reversed the rulings of
previous court actions. The Court viewed the teacher's actions as a right
within the U.S. Constitution. No evidence showed that the teacher's actions
were reckless and disregarding of the truth. The matter was indeed a topic of
public interest, and the school board could not legally dismiss the teacher.

Case #2—*Cleveland Board v. Loudermill* (U.S. Supreme Court, 1981–1986, 470 U.S. 532, 1985). Due Process Rights

Although Loudermill was a classified school employee rather than a teacher, the case has implications for the hiring practices of all school employees. It is common for schools today to require background checks as a hiring procedure. In the case of Loudermill, he was hired as a security guard, and after hiring it was discovered that he had lied on his application about never having been convicted of a felony. Since Loudermill had been hired, by state statute, he had obtained certain property rights. The board did grant him a review, but not until nine months after his termination. Loudermill argued that his rights had been violated since he did not have an opportunity to defend himself before being terminated and that his firing was in violation of his due process rights under the Fourteenth Amendment.

Two other courts considered the case and decided that the board had violated Loudermill's due process rights. Ultimately, the case went to the U.S. Supreme Court. The Court ruled by an 8 to 1 vote that the answer to the question, "Can a state remove a civil servant's rights to employment before providing an opportunity to respond to charges?" was no. Due process before termination is not only required but also it is in the best interests of employees and not a significant administrative burden for the employing agency. The due process of the Fourteenth Amendment required a hearing, and it should be conducted at a meaningful time. The rights and interests of the employee outweighed the state's interests in quickly dismissing employees.

Case #3—*Mt. Healthy City School District Board of Education v. Doyle* (429 U.S. 274, 1977). Denial of Teacher's Tenure

The case was heard by a district court and a court of appeals before going before the U.S. Supreme Court. Dole was a social studies teacher for five years and then learned that his contract had not been renewed. He was being denied tenure and continuing employment in the school district. The school superintendent contended that Doyle made an obscene gesture to students on one occasion and there was an instance when Doyle talked about the school district's dress code with a local radio station. The act in view of the superintendent demonstrated a lack of tact.

Doyle filed a lawsuit against his former school district arguing his rights to free speech. The court ruled in Doyle's favor, and the school district filed an appeal. Ultimately, the U.S. Supreme Court took the case. In brief, the Court ruled that the school district was created by the state and thus was a local case and therefore beyond the reach of the Eleventh Amendment. Although the Supreme Court did not rule regarding the legality of Doyle's termination, it did remand the case to the district court with orders to learn if evidence could be found that would have warranted the firing of Doyle even if he had not contacted the radio station. The result was that the school district was able to demonstrate such evidence in 1982, and so the court upheld the teacher's termination.

The importance of the Mt. Healthy case centers on termination cases whereby the school district must prove that the firing would have taken place even if the protected activity of free speech under the First Amendment had never occurred. The procedure is now referred to as the Mt. Healthy Test.

Case #4—*Island Trees School District Board of Education v. Pico* (457 U.S. 853, 1982). Censorship

Nine books in the school libraries of the school district were viewed as being absolutely unsuitable for junior and senior high school students. The school board directed all school libraries to remove the books from the library shelves. Five students filed a lawsuit on the basis that the board had violated their First Amendment rights of free speech. The case went all the way to the U.S. Supreme Court, which ruled against the school board. In brief, the Court's ruling was based on the opinion that books could not be removed from the school just because the board did not like some of the books' contents. The First Amendment rights of students protect a student's right to learn. Although schools do have the authority to select books for their libraries, they do not have the right to control in a way that tends to repress certain views and opinions that suppress student learning.

Case #5—*Adler v. Board of Education* (342 U.S. 485, 1952). Memberships in Subversive Organizations

A New York law was adopted at the time to protect children from communist influence. The law disqualified public school teachers from employment in the public schools. After being considered by several "inferior courts," it was addressed by the U.S. Supreme Court. The Court was to act on the question as to whether or not such a law was a violation of an individual's freedom of speech and assembly under the First Amendment of the U.S. Constitution. The Court's answer was no. If a person was a member of a subversive organization, the person is not denied the freedom of speech and assembly. By being a member of a subversive organization, the teacher is serving to overthrow the U.S. government by undesirable means. The ruling was not unanimous on the part of the Court. Justice Frankfurter, a dissenter, was of the majority opinion that the Court was being asked to approve a "scheme" that was still an unfinished blueprint. Justice Douglas believed that the Court was approving a law that carried the invidious law of *guilty by association.*

Dissenting Judge Black also disapproved a law that penalized teachers for their beliefs.

Case #6 — *Perry v. Sindermann* (408 U.S. 593, United States Supreme Court, 1972). Teacher Tenure

Although this case involved a teacher in higher education, it holds implications for public school teachers as well. In this case, Sindermann had served as a teacher in the state's college system for several years before becoming a professor in one of the state's junior colleges. Due to his disagreements with policies of the Board of Regents, his contract was not renewed. The Regents alleged insubordination, but a hearing on the case was not held. The court faced the question as to Sindermann's rights of due process under the Fourteenth Amendment, even though he was not on tenure.

The case depended in part on the fact that the college administration had a "de facto" tenure program, and that the plaintiff had the understanding that he had tenure under the more informal program.

Sindermann argued that the college administration had stated that it wanted each faculty member to feel as if he or she had permanent tenure so long as teaching services were satisfactory and the member displayed a cooperative attitude. Sindermann also stated that there had been an understanding that his contract would be renewed.

The key question to be answered centered on whether such informal tenure practices were sufficient to create an entitlement to a hearing on the matter. By a 5 to 3 vote, the Court ruled that Sindermann was entitled to initiate a lawsuit against the college for their decision to terminate him.

Although states commonly have tenure statutes on record, there always seems to be conditions that cause a need for additional review of rights and responsibilities.

Since Sindermann did have considerable time and experience in the system, he did have property rights that had been violated. In the end, the Court ruled that Sindermann had to be given the opportunity to prove his claims in view of the institution's stated policies and current practices. Two Supreme Court judges dissented to the ruling, and one judge, Justice Powell, did not participate in the decision.

Case #7 — *Donohue v. Copiague UFSD* (47 N.Y.2d 440, NY Court of Appeals, 1979). Educational Malpractice

A student filed a suit alleging that his lack of gaining an education was due to the malpractice of school officials. Teachers failed to perform their duties and obligations to educate sufficiently but gave passing grades; failed to interview, discuss, evaluate, or psychologically comprehend and understand such matters; and failed to provide adequate school facilities, teachers, administrators, psychologists, and necessary steps in testing and evaluation for ascertaining the learning needed by the student. The appellant sought damages in the sum of $5,000,000.

The Appellant Court ruled against the claim, stating that making such judgments about educational malpractice would require courts not only to make judgments about the past but also to sit in review of the daily occurrences of school practices and to interfere negatively with the responsibility of local school officials and teachers at the local school level. The U.S. Supreme Court agreed accordingly and stated that the Appellate Division order should be affirmed. Once again, the upper courts left the educational decisions at the state and local school levels.

Case #8—*Elfbrandt v. Russell* (384 U.S. 11, 86 S. CT. 1238, 16 L. Ed. 2d 321, 19676 U.S., 1966). Oaths of Allegiance

The state of Arizona required all public employees to take an oath to support the state and federal constitutions. Those persons that did take the oath became subject to prosecution for perjury and termination if indeed they willingly joined the Communist Party. The plaintiff, Elfbrandt, was a teacher and believed that she could not in good faith take the oath. She claimed that she did not understand the meaning of the oath and that she had not been given a chance to learn its meaning. The question faced by the court was if a state could require all public employees to take such an oath. The U.S. Supreme Court ruled the answer was no. The Court stated that a law that restricts the type of membership that does not have the purpose of furthering illegal objectives inhibits the protection of individual freedom. Such laws suggest that a person is guilty by association, and as such it is unconstitutional.

Case #9—*Hortonville Joint School District No. 1 v. Hortonville Education Association* (U.S. Supreme Court, June 1976). Due Process Required

The school board and teachers' association had negotiated for several months in an attempt to renew a collective bargaining agreement. The teachers were sent letters requesting their return to work without a response. A second letter with the same request also received the same results since striking was against state law. None returned. In follow up, the school board sent each teacher a letter setting forth hearing times for disciplinary hearings. State law prohibited teacher strikes.

The counsel for the teachers informed the school board that the teachers wanted to be treated as a group rather than individually. Teachers argued that the matter should be reviewed by an impartial third party, and the school board did not meet that condition. Due process could not be rendered with the school board in charge. The teachers filed a lawsuit, and the state Supreme Court ruled in favor of the teachers' association. The Court stated that indeed due process required an impartial third party and that fairness could not be achieved if the school board ruled on the matter. However, the case went to the U.S. Supreme Court, and that Court reversed the ruling of the state court.

First of all, the due process clause did not guarantee the teachers an independent review of their termination. In addition, the Court stated that in view of the school board's educational responsibilities for the best interests in the educational program for students, the firing fell within the board's policy of making legal responsibilities. In dismissing the teachers that had violated the state law concerning striking, the firing was within the Board's legislative role as policy makers.

Case #10—*Peter W. v. San Francisco Unified School District* (Court of Appeals of California, First Appellate District, Division Four, August 6, 1976). Inadequate Education Charged

The case at hand centered on the question as to whether an individual who charges that his public education was inadequately provided can file against the public school authorities in charge of the educational system. The court's focus was on the allegations as negligence. The plaintiff claimed that the school district negligently failed to provide adequate instruction, guidance, counseling, and supervision in the basic academic skills. Negligence was evident in the school district's failure to use proper care in the discharge of its responsibilities to provide the plaintiff with adequate instruction and did not demonstrate a satisfactory degree of professionalism required by a competent educator. In its ruling in favor of the defendant, the court found no cause of action for negligence on the part of the school district.

The record of this case is lengthy but especially important as well. It is beyond our purposes here to detail the decision factors of the case in more detail. However, the following court's statement does give further perspective of the court's rationale for its ruling favoring education officials in cases of schools being sued for the inadequate education of students. As the court stated:

> Unlike the activity of the highway or the market place, classroom methodology affords no readily acceptable standards of care, or cause, or injury. The science of pedagogy itself is fraught with different and conflicting theories of how or what a child should be taught, and any layman might—and commonly—does have his own emphatic views on the subject. The "injury" claimed here is plaintiff's inability to read and write. Substantial professional authority attests that the achievement of literacy in the schools, or its failure, are influ-

enced by a host of factors which affect the pupil subjectively, from outside the formal teaching process, and beyond the control of its ministers. They may be physical, neurological, emotional, cultural, environmental; they may be present but not perceived, recognized but not identified.

LEGAL CONSIDERATIONS CONCERNING THE HIRING OF TEACHER PERSONNEL

School employees are entitled to statutory rights and contractual rights. *Statutory rights* are those protections set forth by governmental agencies such as those laws by state legislatures. *Contractual rights* are based on contract law. Courts have held consistently that teaching licenses are not contracts.

A contract between a school board and an administrator or teacher has the same contingencies as contracts between other individuals or business parties. A valid contract commonly is considered to possess five key elements: capacity, offer, consideration, acceptance, and mutuality. *Capacity* refers to the authority of the parties to contract. An *offer* consists of an agreement to do something or to refrain from doing something. It is a specified action. *Consideration* refers to the fact that the offer has to be something of value in exchange for a specific action or nonaction. It would not be a legally binding contract if one party did all of the offering without a commensurate return of adequate value given by the other party. Both parties must be in *acceptance* of the specified terms of the contract. There must be a meeting of the minds whereby both parties are in agreement with the terms. To understand and agree with the terms of the contract is viewed as *mutuality.*

The data gathered from the legal survey reported in chapter 2 indicated that teacher hiring was viewed as a serious or difficult legal issue or problem by two-thirds of the participating school principals. If there is a problem and a lawsuit is likely to be filed by one of the two parties, sometimes there are set terms for doing so. For example, in the case of oral contracts, a common term for filing a lawsuit is four years. A written contract filing term commonly is six years. When the contract deals with the sale of goods, the common term to file is four years, since teacher contracts commonly are for one year only and are accompanied by the state's tenure laws. Peterson and others (1978) point out that a school district has no inherent power to contract. That is, a school board must look to the state legislature for all of its powers. Additionally, a school district must act through the school board. A local school cannot contract for goods or services on its own volition. In addition, with the possible exception of the state of Connecticut, only the school board can officially hire a teacher.

To be valid, school boards must act within the state's statutes for contracting services. In any case, the school board must commit to the stipulations of state statutes for contracting services, including the services of administrators and teachers. For example, if a state statute indicates that all teacher hires must be officially licensed to teach in the public schools of the state, the school board cannot hire a teacher officially pending the receipt of a teaching certificate/license. If, for example, the state statues specify that there is a minimum age limit for a teacher, the underage teacher lacks the authority to contract. In some cases, the underage teacher can have an authorized adult sign the contract on his or her behalf.

A teacher is required to teach the grades and the subjects as specified in the signed contract. That is, if an elementary school teacher signed a contract that indicated that she was hired as a third-grade teacher, he or she could not be assigned to teach another grade unless the teacher agrees to do so. If the teacher were contracted to teach in the primary grades, he or she could be assigned to teach in any one of the grades 1 or 2 depending, of course, on the state's categorization of the grades in each of the primary, middle, and upper elementary grade levels. Similarly, a secondary school teacher that was hired by contract to teach mathematics could not be assigned to teach a science subject without his or her agreement to do so.

The assignment to teach in the school district does, however, give the school administration the authority to place the teacher in any school within the school district that has the grade(s) or subject(s) that the contract set forth. It should be noted that both school district policies and the state's legal statutes are part of the teacher's contract, and that school officials are wise to discuss these "rules" with the teacher candidate before actual hiring takes place. A thorough knowledge of such rules should be attended upon the teacher's employment. Failure to do so can result in unwanted legal problems and is commonly viewed by the courts as negligence on the part of school personnel.

ADDITIONAL THOUGHTS REGARDING TEACHING ASSIGNMENTS

Give thought to a situation in which a teacher's personal beliefs are contrary to such controversial subjects as abortion, gay rights, same-sex marriages, Islamic studies, and so forth. Does he or she have any recourse if those topics are required in the curriculum or course of study to which they are assigned? Simplistically, one might argue that the teacher has the right to request a different teaching assignment. However, if the teacher's contract assigns him or her to teach a certain subject area and the state and school board have required these controversial subjects to be taught in the school curriculum, refusal to do so certainly would be considered as insubordination. Objective teaching of these subjects would be required in the same manner that teaching about the history of a religion(s) objectively is not a constitutional violation; that is, teaching about a religion rather than teaching and/or supporting a specific religious point of view.

To what extent do the suggestions or requirements in a teacher's professional improvement plan developed as a result of an unsatisfactory evaluation/observation have to be met in order to be retained as a teacher, or conversely, be dismissed? It seems clear that if the teacher's improvement plan called for specific improvement and school officials had evidence that substantial needed improvement support had been given the teacher without successful results, this evidence would be viewed as being sufficient for dismissal. Of course, due process rights in such cases, especially for tenured personnel, would be important. The statutory procedures of giving notice to the teacher of the alleged grounds for dismissal must be followed (Peterson et al., 1978, p. 448).

Even though teacher contracts commonly are based on examples supplied by the state or drafted by the school district's legal counsel, several key factors facilitate the drafting of clearly written and understandable contracts. Peterson and others (1978) set forth several factors that are found in effective contracts and serve to minimize misinterpretation and lawsuits that can result otherwise:

1. The terms of the contract are clear and unmistakable.
2. If the terms of the contract are not clear on their face, evidence is admissible to clarify them.
3. Oral understandings should be "merged" in the written agreement.
4. If a teacher receives a contract that has been signed by the school board and he or she has objections to it, the contract should be returned with a statement of the objections.
5. Doubts in a contract can be resolved but are commonly resolved by the party that writes the contract.
6. Handwritten and typed provisions take precedent over printed matter in the contract.
7. Most generally, the terms of a contract can extend beyond the terms of the succeeding board.
8. Valid contractual agreements are most commonly binding by the approval of the school board as a whole.
9. A legal contract is valid for the entire time set forth in the contract, not just for the time remaining after it is signed. (pp. 137–38)

LEGAL CONSIDERATIONS FOR HIRING: INTERVIEWING NO-NO'S

To avoid potential litigation when hiring personnel, school interviewers must be fully aware of employment laws and the interview techniques that avoid charges of discrimination. At this time in history, it would seem unnecessary to worry about someone not knowing the "rules" about interview questioning set forth by the Equal Employment Opportunity Commission (EEOC). Nevertheless, even experienced administrators and teachers that participate in the hiring process have been known to violate EEOC employment practices that govern employment.

We submit that the no-no's of questioning applicants about certain matters such as criminal records and sexual conduct tend to be confusing. Authorities on the matter of interviewing are quick to point out that questions such as "Have you ever been arrested or convicted of a crime?" is an inappropriate question to ask in a teacher interview. Yet most everyone accepts the need for a background check that commonly focuses directly on the candidate's criminal record.

Although background checks on potential hires are commonplace, asking a teacher candidate, "Have you ever been convicted of a felony?" could be considered as discriminatory. The answer appears to be vested in the question, "What would be an acceptable reason for asking the question?" If an applicant does have a past criminal record, is this a legal cause for not considering the applicant for a teaching position? It appears that school districts have the right to turn down applicants with criminal records whether or not such hiring is forbidden by state law. It is certain that numerous school districts have "unknowingly" hired felons for school positions. Reportedly, one school district learned that it had hired seven felons and summarily fired them after learning about it. It does not make sense to mandate background checks unless there is a hiring reason for doing so.

The matter of legality and asking certain questions is problematic. States differ in their statutes but tend to leave decisions about hiring to local school boards. One principle to follow in establishing interview questions for teacher applicants is to be sure that the question asked has a basis of reason for the position in question. For example, it seems reasonable to learn if a teacher candidate has a history of child sex abuse. What about smoking? Although smoking in itself would not be an acceptable reason for not hiring a teacher, informing a smoker of a school's regulation against smoking anywhere at any time on school property appears to be of importance. This consideration applies to the hiring of classified personnel as well.

One situation involved the rejection of a blind applicant for a position in the school cafeteria that necessitated the selling of snacks and beverages. The reason given the EEOC, of course, was that the applicant was blind and incapable of handling the merchandise and money transactions that were essential in the position. The EEOC asked for specific evidence that the school officials' contention was true in fact. The blind applicant was hired and reportedly handled the required tasks exceptionally well.

REDUCTION IN FORCE

It seems somewhat pretentious to consider the matter of reduction of force when so many schools nationally are in need of teacher personnel. It seems that no one becomes too concerned about reduction in force (RIF) until conditions actually warrant such actions. Yet with major budgetary cuts in educational support, the matter of releasing teachers from contracts is a reality in today's economic climate. Prior to any specific legislation concerning the need to cut teaching forces, school districts locally tended to use the need to reduce the size of the teaching staff as a means of releasing marginal teachers and retaining teachers with high-quality evaluations. However, in the middle 1960s to late 1960s, many states passed legislation to direct the release of personnel when various factors brought about the need to cut school expenditures. As a result, most every legislative act relating to a reduction in force in education followed the model of business and industry for handling the problem.

Seniority was ruled the procedure for determining first to last releases from duty. In fact, the term *unrequested leave of absence* became appropriate for defining the right of recall of teachers in case of RIF procedures. That is, state statutes set the procedures for cutting staff sizes educationally. Three conditions are the paramount reasons of RIF implementation: the school district's financial condition due to such factors as the school reorganization, severe budgetary allocations, or decreases in student enrollment. Eventually, the factors of seniority and performance evaluation results were used in implementing unrequested leaves of absence.

As previously noted, teachers who are subject to RIF have the right of recall. In most cases, the RIF procedures apply to both tenured and probationary teachers. In cases of complaint, the law commonly provided the right to a hearing. Such a right commonly applies to both tenured and probationary teachers. Whether or not the released teacher has the right to continue health insurance coverage and other benefits depends solely on the state's statutes and actions of the local school board.

TEACHER DISMISSAL

Teacher personnel enjoy certain rights of all citizens relating to freedom of speech, nondiscrimination, and other protections related to suspension and dismissal. The U.S. Constitution establishes many of these rights, and state and federal laws and statutes give other protections. Such violations as insubordination, incompetency, willful neglect of duty, conviction of a crime, or knowingly failing to report suspected child abuse are among the behaviors viewed as misconduct in office. Today, dismissal continues to be a difficult legal matter.

Teacher dismissal was viewed as a serious or difficult legal problem by approximately two-thirds of the school principals in the principal survey presented in chapter 2. It is common practice for teacher personnel to gain property rights after serving satisfactorily for three years as a classroom teacher. Thus, certain specific procedures are set forth in state statutes in dealing with the dismissal of a tenured teacher. *Tenure* is defined as the protection given to teachers against arbitrary dismissal. Nontenured teachers commonly do not have similar dismissal rights. In some states, school boards can refuse to issue a contract of a nontenured teacher during any one of the first three years of service. In addition, courts have ruled that school boards do not have to set forth a list of reasons as to why the teacher is not being rehired. This is not the case for tenured personnel.

A tenured teacher in one school district in a state that moves to another school district in the same state does not always receive automatic tenure in the new school district. These cases tend to be handled differently. For example, in one state, a tenured teacher in the state that moves to another state public school is given tenure after if his or her contract is renewed after one year of probationary employment under certain conditions; for example, the new teacher's last performance evaluation from the district in which he or she was formerly employed was satisfactory or better, or there is no break in the new employee's service between the two systems of more than one year. Other contingencies commonly do apply as well.

A related situation centers on the condition of tenure when a school district undergoes consolidation. In such cases, courts have ruled that a teacher that has been tenured in the original district does not lose tenure as a result of the consolidation and is entitled to all of the tenure benefits that were enjoyed in the original district (*Hensley v. State Board of Education*, 1962).

It is common today for states and local school boards to require performance evaluation programs for probationary teachers and tenured teachers as well. In the case of probationary teachers, if the probationary teacher is not doing satisfactory work toward qualifying for tenure, a mentor is assigned and an individual performance improvement plan is required. The mentoring program must be based on established standards for effective mentoring.

Dismissal of a tenured teacher is one of the most difficult and traumatic personnel actions that school administrators must face. One study found that personnel directors viewed dismissing incompetent staff among the list of the ten most difficult problems facing them (Norton, 2004). However, dismissal is not a new phenomenon. Nearly one hundred years ago two authorities described the seriousness of worker dismissals (Tead & Metcalf, 1920). As these persons noted, dismissal involved a serious dislocation of one's life, the uprooting of the person's home and his or her children's schooling, and most likely a serious decrease in resources for the person's family. It must be regarded as a serious matter.

It is clear that a teacher cannot be suspended or dismissed for exercising a constitutional right. This fact was settled nearly fifty years ago by the ruling of the U.S. Supreme Court in 1968. In the case of *Pickering v. the Board of Education*, a high school teacher was dismissed for criticizing the district's Board of Education for the way it handled its proposals for raising funding for district schools. Pickering claimed that his rights of free speech and due process had been violated. Pickering had criticized the school board's handling of the bond issue but also criticized its allocation of monetary funding in regard to education and athletic programs. In addition, Pickering claimed that the school superintendent was attempting to prevent teachers from taking a stand against the bond issue.

The Supreme Court of Illinois confirmed Pickering's dismissal. The case went to the highest court of the United States, and the Court ruled that the dismissal of a public school teacher for public statements regarding issues of public importance without showing that the statements were knowingly or recklessly false violated the First Amendment rights of free speech. Thus the Court reversed the previous ruling of the District Court.

It is true that "reckless" disregard for the truth does not protect an individual by law. Although employees do have the right to criticize their superiors and the Board of Education, such criticism cannot be false or reckless. In addition, however, dismissal of a teacher for violations sets forth in the state's tenure laws is permissible if indeed the violations can be proven.

TEACHER INSUBORDINATION

"I understand your position on the matter, Principal Romero, but as a professional I am absolutely opposed to your position and want you to know that I have not been willing to implement your mandate and will continue to oppose doing so." Or, "I understand your position on the matter, Principal Romero, but as a professional I personally cannot agree with the mandate but I have reluctantly implemented the mandate and will continue to do so." In regard to teacher insubordination, although somewhat similar, the two contentions are quite different in regard to insubordinate behaviors.

In the first case above, the teacher has not supported the principal's orders and has not implemented the procedures set forth, nor does the teacher plan to do so. This behavior in most every court would be a cause of insubordination and potential suspension or dismissal. On the other hand, although the teacher in the second case is opposed to the principal's order, the teacher has obeyed the order by implementing it in practice. In addition, the teacher agrees to continue to support the order of the mandate until possible changes are made in its provisions. The teacher has shown no disrespect of the school principal in disagreeing with the orders set forth. In neither case did the teacher use rude, vulgar, or inappropriate behaviors.

Pryor (2015, June 30) points out that insubordination is the act of willfully disobeying an authority figure: "the typical way an employee gets into trouble for insubordination by refusing to perform an action that their supervisor, or other authority figure, requests" (p. 2). It is wise for an employee to perform a particular work duty when it is explicit and clearly given. Nevertheless, it is not insubordination to refuse an act that is unethical or illegal regardless who requests it.

Insubordination has been ruled for numerous other teacher behaviors. For example, in one case a teacher refused to allow supervisory personnel to enter his classroom. The court ruled that dismissal was justified. In other cases, teachers were dismissed for refusing to complete forms to be used in the evaluation of school departments. A teacher that distributed flyers against school board policy was dismissed. A teacher was dismissed for refusal to comply with the school board's requirement to take an annual physical examination. Perhaps one of the most unusual cases of insubordination was that of a teacher that was absent from school for reasons of illness. However, the teacher was seen walking and then refused to explain the situation or to present evidence of his illness. By court ruling, the charge of dismissal for insubordination was upheld (Peterson et al., 1978).

Snapshot 3.1 I'm the Professional and Have My Own Ideas of Teaching Effectiveness

Elmer Bumgardner was a math teacher at Wymore Middle School. He had taught in the same school district for sixteen years but asked for transfer to a new middle school that was located closer to his home. He had been a teacher at the Wymore Middle School for three years. Elmer had trouble dealing cordially with parents and reportedly had little patience with slow learners. During his second year at the middle school, his annual performance rating was satisfactory on all evaluation criteria except knowledge of the subject curriculum, which was rated as being "above average." That is the performance evaluation scale including ratings of 1, Excellent; 2, Very Good; 3, Good; 4, Fair; and 5, Poor.

It was clear at the outset of Elmer's work in the school that, as he put it, "I'm my own man." He commonly came late to faculty meetings with the excuse that "I had to stay with some of my students who needed some after-school attention." One parent complained to the school principal that Mr. Bumgardner had just walked away when she approached him and asked about his "treatment" of her son in the classroom. As Mr. Bumgardner explained to the principal, "I'm here to present mathematics and not to have to contend with unruly kids or patronizing parents."

Members of the school board on more than one occasion had contacted the school superintendent about personal calls that they had received on Bumgardner's unsatisfactory parental and student relationships. The board president gave the strong opinion that something had to be done about this matter. As a result of the increasing criticism of Bumgardner's reported behavior, Superintendent Fredstrom asked Principal Johnson to meet with him on the matter of Bumgardner and his continuation as a teacher in the school district.

Principal Johnson agreed with the superintendent that the matter had gotten out of hand and that indeed something had to be done.

"I have tried more times than I can recall to get this teacher to get along with others and to follow the school district's math curriculum. He just doesn't seem to listen and responds by saying, 'Is that all?'"

It was decided to conduct a hearing whereby the board would be able to present evidence and the teacher would be able to present his story.

"Let's just state that Mr. Bumgardner does not meet the professional growth requirements of the school district and does not meet the instructional qualifications desired in the school and the Wymore School District," recommended Superintendent Fredstrom.

At the formal hearing, Superintendent Fredstrom did just as he had recommended. He underscored the information that Mr. Bumgardner did not meet the professional requirements expected of a Wymore schoolteacher in both his personal behavior and his classroom performance.

At one point, the hearing officer asked about Bumgardner's teaching performance. Principal Johnson used the overhead projector to show the teacher's ratings. On a scale of 1 low and 5 high, Mr. Bumgardner had received evaluation scores of all 3s and one score of 2.

As additional evidence, the hearing officer asked Mr. Bumgardner to report his professional development activities over the last three years. In brief, the school district's requirements for professional growth were for teachers on tenure to earn six college credits in their subject matter or major degree area each four years.

Discussion: Assume the role of the hearing officer in Snapshot #3.1 and give your "ruling" or recommendation for the case with the information/evidence provided in Snapshot 3.1. Write a brief summary of one paragraph that sets forth your observations and recommended rulings in the Bumgardner case. You need to give special attention to the actual "evidence" that was presented by the school officials and by the teacher. Set aside your subjective opinions about Bumgardner and his behaviors. Focus on the known facts as presented at the hearing. As hearing officer, what are your findings, recommendations, and rulings regarding your report back to the school board?

A study was conducted that examined court cases about adverse employment actions against public educators for insubordination. The cases that were included in the study were those spanning the years from early 1900 to 2011 (O'Neal, 2014). The stated purpose of the study was to understand what courts consider to be insubordination. Only insubordination of teachers and principals was studied. Of the 129 cases that were briefed, only 27.9 percent were ruled in favor of the teacher or principal. In regard to insubordinate charges, 50.4 percent centered on cases involving the educator's inability to follow board policy, direct orders, or directives from superiors. In the legal principal survey discussed in chapter 2, approximately 20 percent of the participating school principals expressed the opinion that insubordination was a "serious" issue for them; approximately 40 percent viewed it as being "difficult."

It is quite clear that an employee's absolute refusal to follow directives from superiors is viewed as an insubordinate behavior. However, this fact does not set aside the employee's right to question an order or to suggest that an unwise order should be reconsidered. The teacher has the freedom of speech to ask questions about a directive or to strongly recommend that an action is not in the best interests of students. However, disobeying a direct order, unless the order would be injurious to the party or other individuals, would be viewed by the court as insubordination. It is clear that disobeying a nondiscriminatory order or regulation by a governmental authority that has its authority vested in the purpose of public good and safety would be ruled as insubordination.

The landmark case of *Pickering v. Board of Education* (1968) has had far-reaching effects on a teacher's freedom to speak. As stated by the U.S. Supreme Court, "Absent proof of false statements knowingly or recklessly made by him, a teacher's exercise of his right to speak on issues of public importance may not furnish the basis for his dismissal from public employment."

Revocation of administrator or teacher licenses is another legal matter. Grounds for the revocation of educator licenses have included such reasons as mental illness, cheating on the recertification examination, willful violation of state law, illicit relations with a female student, drunkenness, and immoral or unprofessional conduct. However, reportedly the most common grounds for a revocation of license are immoral activities and unprofessional conduct or incompetence (Peterson et al., 1978).

It is interesting to note the matter of dress code as it applies to faculty personnel. In the legal principal survey introduced in chapter 2, faculty dress code loomed as a difficult issue/problem for 29.8 percent of the school principals. However, another 11.5 percent viewed faculty dress as a serious legal matter in their schools.

BREACHES OF TEACHER CONTRACTS

As is the case with contracts in general, a breach of contract can occur on actions of the employee or the school board. Breaches of contract commonly occur when a teacher has taken an unauthorized leave or resigns before the contract terms are completed. If a teacher is terminated before the end of the contract and the teacher has not violated the terms, the school board most likely will be accused of breaching the contract. In any case, the provisions of the teacher's contract determine whether or not a contract has been breached.

Although nearly two-thirds of the school principals in the previously mentioned legal survey stated that teacher insubordination was "no problem" for them, the other one-third viewed it as serious or difficult. When a teacher leaves a position before the end of the contract term, the educational results for students can be damaging. Just hiring another replacement seldom assures the continuation of a quality instructional program for students. In one case, an art teacher was offered a "prestigious" position as director of a university art museum. The teacher insisted that he be released to take advantage of the position offering and stated that he would resign in any case. The school board approved the teacher's termination, and another certified art teacher was hired to complete the last school semester. No other art candidates were available at midyear. Reportedly, the teacher replacement's performance proved to be unsatisfactory. The "new" teacher was not rehired for the next school year.

The school board questioned its own judgment regarding their release from the contract of the first art teacher. If, indeed, it was the school board's responsibility to assure the best possible instructional program for students, was it wise to release a quality art teacher for a marginal teacher for one entire school semester? Some school officials argued that not releasing the teacher would have meant keeping a teacher on the job that did not want to be there. The assistant superintendent of schools, who originally recommended that the present art teacher be required to complete the present school term, felt otherwise. He argued that a professional teacher under these circumstances would have continued to do quality instruction regardless of his eagerness to assume the position at the local university.

In some cases, the teacher's contract stipulates the monetary damages when a teacher resigns before the term of the contract. If this is not the case, damages caused by the early resignation most likely would have to be decided by a court. Minimally, the school board would incur the expenses of hiring a teacher replacement. On the other hand, if the school board breaches a teacher's contract, the damages commonly are determined monetarily by the amount of money that the teacher would have received if he or she continued as a teacher. In addition, other costs related to finding new employment most likely would be refunded.

There are specified procedures that any public school employee can implement if he or she wishes to be released from the contract. The employee commonly sends a letter to the school board with the time of the release and the reasons for the request specifically stated. If approved by the school board, the employee is released from the position and the contract is considered to be null and void by the specified date set forth by the school board. Breaching of the employee contract by the employee is most serious and can result in suspension for a specified period of time, with the possible loss of licensure for the position in question.

LEGAL CONSIDERATIONS REGARDING AGE OF TEACHERS AND ADMINISTRATORS

Teacher age has been more of a legal problem than most would expect. Rosales (2012) has cited several cases whereby age has been contended. For example, in one instance a teacher was denied a promotion to assistant principal because of her age. As a result, the Equal Employment Opportunity Commission (EEOC) filed an amicus brief (strong interest in the case but not a party to the action) stating that the court should not dismiss a discrimination suit against the school board. In addition, it has been reported that numerous age discrimination suits have been filed whereby school administrators have been dismissed because of their age.

Age Discrimination in Employment Act of 1967 provides age protection. The Act stipulates that age discrimination cannot be the sole factor for the termination of employment. In addition, those teachers age forty and over are protected against age discrimination. If termination of a person over forty is recommended, age cannot be the only reason for such action. The age discrimination law is comprehensive in that it focuses on the human resource processes of hiring, position assignments, professional development, compensation, promotion, and termination.

Discrimination in regard to early retirement procedures is also of legal concern. That is, early retirement incentive plans that discriminate on the basis of age are illegal (Rosales, 2012).

WHAT ABOUT LEGAL RESPONSIBILITIES IN REGARD TO OFF-CAMPUS ACTIVITIES SUCH AS CLASS FIELD TRIPS?

The significance of being an invitee or licensee in relation to a school activity such as a field trip was discussed previously in the chapter. Sindelar (2015, June 30) points out that to hold a teacher or administrator liable for injury, the student must provide evidence that proves four things: (1) the teacher had a duty to be careful to not injure the student and thus to protect the student from harm, (2) the teacher did not use due care in view of the activity pursued, (3) the teacher's lack of care was responsible for the student's injury, and (4) the student did sustain actual injury during the activity such as a field trip. Furthermore, Sindelar underscores the fact that, contrary to an erroneous belief, a parental permission slip or even a parental waiver does not release the teacher in charge from negligence and personal responsibility.

Nevertheless, a signed permission slip does provide some evidence that the teacher has given thought to the field trip in mind and that he or she is acting in a caring manner. Some courts have enforced the concept of in loco parentis in regard to activities such as field trip activities. That is, the teacher has the authority to act as the students' parents and enforce rules as would be done within the school classroom. Teacher negligence in these instances most always results in teacher liability. That is, the teacher has not demonstrated the ability of a prudent teacher needed in the exercise of ordinary care to foresee the harmful effects that will follow commission of some act. In short, the teacher has not exercised ordinary care in relation to the activity pursued. A teacher is always personally liable for his or her negligence. The point here is that, although the entire issue of administrator and teacher is extremely involved and requires the services of legal counsel, it is incumbent on them to be well versed in matters of legal responsibilities and liabilities of their relationships with student personnel.

LEGAL RULINGS IN THE AREA OF PUBLIC SCHOOL INSTRUCTION

It seems clear that public schools cannot include any activities or programs that include the teaching of a religion. In addition, any subversive instruction in public schools is forbidden. It is also clear that the state has the authority as to what is taught in America's classrooms, although state authority commonly is delegated to the local school's Board of Education. In fact, early court cases established the fact that when the state requires certain subjects to be taught in public schools, local school boards must offer the subjects. When the state does not have a directive statute on a particular curricular subject, it generally is understood that the local school board is able to determine what is to be done educationally. As previously noted in this chapter, many school policies are based on "verbatim statements" of approved state statutes. It is interesting to note that course subjects have been challenged regarding their inclusion in the school program. Nevertheless, courts have upheld school boards' authority to offer such courses as foreign language, certain arts programs, dramatics, dance programs, and others.

Peterson and others (1978) have pointed out that one of the most controversial curricular subjects in recent history has been sex education. In brief, the courts have supported the school's right to offer such courses, but in some cases have so ruled if the course was not compulsory. Once again, courts have demonstrated their reluctance to engage in educational matters that are best determined by the local school district. The topics of girls' sports participation, programs for drivers' education, kindergarten programs, age restriction for athletic participation, school dances, physical education participation, and others have been topics of court cases historically.

The federal government's concern for the public school educational program is clear as well. In previous chapters we have underscored the federal government's influence on the school curriculum in such areas as mathematics and science, agriculture, foreign language, physical education, special education, school inclusiveness, and other program areas. Federal influence, however, almost always is accompanied by the withholding of federal funds if certain program provisions are not implemented.

Court cases historically have determined what can or cannot be taught in public schools. An early example of this fact is demonstrated by the case of the *State v. John Scopes* (1925). Scopes, a high school science teacher, was arrested and charged with teaching the theory of evolution. At the close of this famous trial, a verdict of guilty was ruled. Some forty-three years later, the U.S. Supreme Court unanimously ruled that the law that banned the teaching of evolution was unconstitutional and violated the Establishment Clause of the First Amendment that centers on prohibiting the establishment of a religion in schools.

BACKGROUND CHECKS FOR SCHOOL EMPLOYEES

Criminal background checks commonly are required for all personnel when hiring school employees for professional and classified school positions. The requirement applies to substitute teachers as well. Background checks among the states do vary. In some cases the background check centers primarily on the candidate's criminal record. "Estimates indicate that up to 40% of applicant resumes contain false or tweaked information. Cases of hiring personnel who did not have the required credentials for the position in question, who had not reported past records of child molestation or other criminal activities, who submitted false information concerning their previous work history, or who reported other erroneous information on the job applications have made comprehensive background checks a requirement in almost every school district nationally" (Norton, 2008, p. 143).

A comprehensive background check can include the candidate's entire work experience and complete criminal record. Checking the candidate's credit report is somewhat controversial. Nevertheless, if asking for the candidate's credit report has some importance for the position in question, this appears as an acceptable rationale for doing so. Schools officials can ask for an applicant's academic records, but in most cases the applicant must give permission for the school to do so. A key point appears to be that certain records cannot be requested or obtained unless the information is relevant to the position in question. Asking a teacher candidate for an official college transcript is most appropriate in the eyes of the teaching profession.

It is not legal for school officials to request the medical records of applicants. If medical information is necessary concerning the applicant's ability to do the work required, the school can ask for medical records. However, the school district cannot discriminate against a candidate on the basis of his or her disability or medical condition. In fact, the EEOC will likely ask the school officials to present evidence that the medical information or disability will prohibit the applicant from performing effectively in the job.

It is important that a background check be compliant with the Fair Credit Reporting Act (FCRA) of 1969. If not, there are certain restrictions as to the information that can be collected. The Act is a United Federal Law codified at Title 15, U.S. Code Section 1681.

CONTROVERSY AND THE COMMON CORE STANDARDS

Curriculum mandates were viewed as serious or difficult issues/problems by 87.5 percent of the principals reporting in the aforementioned legal principal study. Common Core Standards would be considered as a major part of curriculum concerns.

In 2015, the matter of Common Core Standards for public school curriculum was a topic of national controversy. In fact, a lawsuit filed against the standards by Governor Bobby Jindal of Louisiana was scheduled to be heard that year. Jindal expressed the opinion that the federal government (President Obama's administration) had forced Louisiana and other states to adopt the Common Core curriculum when they tailored the requirements for federal education grant money and waivers to the Common Core academic standards. The concern centered on the opinion that the federal government was interfering with an educational matter that was historically under the jurisdiction of the states.

In 2014, Governor Jindal lost at state court whereby a judge ruled that he must stop blocking the state's purchase and use of Common Core tests.

As would be expected, numerous articles have been published on the pros and cons of the Common Core Standards. Besides the pending court case in which Jindal is suing the Obama administration over the Common Core Standards, other court cases will appear most likely in the months ahead. We have examined many articles that have set forth reasons that the Common Core Standards should or should not be supported. In the following section, potential legal opinions/contentions that might reach the courts are briefed. Understand that the entries expressed are taken at random from various publications on the topic and do not necessarily express the opinions of me or the publisher of this book. Rather, the purpose here is to point out possible legal suits that could reach various courts in the United States of America.

1. The matter of which governmental body is in the best position and has the legal authority to determine what should be taught in the public schools. The program violates the Constitution of the United States.
2. The high cost of implementing the Common Core Standards seems to rest on the states. The cost of the implementation of the standards far outweighs their potential for improving student learning.
3. The testing procedures and personal information collected throughout the program is an invasion of privacy.
4. The requirements of Common Core undermine the historical concept of local control of education. It fosters a national curriculum that militates against parental and community values that have directed school programs historically.
5. Have the Common Core Standards truly been state led, or are they "mandates" established by a federal initiative supported by the presidential office of the United States?
6. In a direct way, Common Core Standards militate against the freedom of teachers to teach in the classroom.
7. The Common Core Standards reportedly will fix the "wrongs" of current school programs.
8. The contention that the Common Core Standards are internationally benchmarked is flawed and without scientific support.
9. The Common Core program must be stopped since it is based on far too many academic flaws.
10. The Common Core Standards were developed undemocratically and "forced" upon the nation's schools unilaterally.

A POSITIVE PERSPECTIVE OF THE COMMON CORE STANDARDS

Support of the Common Core Standards has been as extensive as its nonsupport. We selected a positive response written by Porter-Magee and Stern (2015, July 2) to underscore the "other side of the story." In their article titled "Why Are Prominent Conservatives Criticizing a Set of Rigorous Educational Standards?" these members of the Thomas B. Fordham Institute make the following observations.

1. The core standards are not a curriculum; rather, they compare with existing state standards that can be used to choose curricula locally that comply with the standards.
2. Common Core is not "ObamaCore," but it was initiated long before he took office in 2009.
3. Education funding is still within the purview of the states; only about 10 percent of a school district's funding comes from the federal government.
4. Contrary to popular belief, English teachers are not required to devote 70 percent of their total reading time to informational texts.
5. Common Core Standards simply delineate what children should know at each grade level and describe the skills that they must have to choose curricula that comply with the standards.
6. Perhaps the clearest evidence that states can still set their own standards is the fact that five states have not adopted Common Core.
7. The Common Core Standards are a floor as opposed to a ceiling. Therefore, there is ample opportunity for local schools to set higher standards.
8. When Common Core was examined and compared to state standards, it found for most states that Common Core is a great improvement with regard to rigor and cohesiveness. (pp. 1–6)

Once again, it is interesting to note the possible lawsuits and court rulings that might be the topics under review. Recall our purposes for the foregoing discussion. Current education problems hold high potential of being addressed in legal courts of law. If the following questions were posed and being considered by the U.S. Supreme Court, what opinion would you select as the one most likely decided by the Court?

Local Schools of America (LSA) v. State: Can the federal office of the U.S. presidency withhold federal funds to a state that does not adopt programs such as Common Core?

Potential Rulings:

a. School program/curricular provisions are the responsibility of the states by the Establishment Clause of the U.S. Constitution. Ruling in favor of the Plaintiff.
b. The U.S. Constitution states that its most important responsibility is vested in protecting the best interests and welfare of the citizenry. The education of the citizenry looms large as a concern of the federal government. Overseeing the quality of education therefore is a function of the federal government and those elected to govern the country. Ruling in favor of the Defendant.
c. Education by Constitution is a responsibility of the states. The case of the *Local Schools of America v. State* therefore is a state problem and the case is remanded to the Supreme Courts of each state.

KEY IDEAS AND RECOMMENDATIONS SET FORTH IN CHAPTER 3

- *The Personnel Function Is a Large Part of a School Administrator's and Teachers' Legal World*: The personnel function in public schools is a major player in the legal responsibilities and liabilities of public schools.
- *Teachers' Rights Are Protected as Citizens of the United States*: Administrators and teachers are protected in their professional positions similarly to their protections as a citizen of the United States.
- *Freedom of Speech Does Not Protect Certain Behaviors of Insubordination*: Insubordination is a serious legal offense on the part of teacher personnel, but their freedom of speech is protected by the U.S. Constitution for stating their opinions on professional matters when done in a truthful and reasonable manner.
- *Knowledge of Due Process Provisions Is an Essential Legal Requirement for School Leaders*: Virtually every case contended in the area of personnel points out the vital importance of implementing due process procedures.
- *Charges and Claims of Violations Must Be Accompanied by Proof in Evidence*: In personnel court cases and personnel hearings, the ability to show evidence that proves the charges set forth is crucial.
- *Employee Seniority Is a Major Factor in the Implementation of RIF*: Reduction in force procedures most commonly are set forth in state statues and must be followed to the letter.
- *Teacher Suspension and Dismissal Are to Be Implemented by Procedures Set Forth in State Statutes*: Teacher suspension and dismissal procedures as set forth in state statutes and school board policies must be followed in all instances. Failure to follow the law is tantamount to losing the school's case in court.

- *School Board Policies and Administrative Regulations Are Part of a Teacher's Contract and So Teachers Should Be Knowledgeable of the Policies Affecting Them*: The teacher's contract can be breached by either the teacher or the board of education. Teachers and administrators must become knowledgeable about contract provisions and those actions and behaviors that lead to contract breaches.
- *Age Discrimination Is Illegal*: Hiring, dismissal, promotion, compensation, or other personnel processes are discriminatory if based on age.
- *The State Is the Legal Authority Relative to School Curricula*: Although teachers have certain autonomy relative to teaching strategies and methodology, they are required to teach the curriculum as set forth in state statutes and by the Board of Education.
- *Negligence Leads to Being Held Responsible for Injuries*: Negligence during school activities off campus leaves the schoolteacher or other supervisor liable for accidents that lead to student injuries.
- *Employee Background Checks Have Proven to Be of Great Importance*: Employee background checks are not only needed in regard to the hiring of public school personnel, but they most often are required by state statute.
- *Common Core Requirements Continue to Be Problematic*: The matter of adoption of the Common Core Standards reportedly has been accepted by nearly all fifty states. Nevertheless, their legal status remains in question. Schools can expect to witness additional court rulings due to the ongoing criticisms of the Common Core provisions.
- *Field Trips and Other Activities Have the Potential for Student Injuries and Liable Outcomes*: An invitee designation has some advantage over a licensee since the owner must take special steps to care for the safety of invitees. Negligence or carelessness can result in a teacher's liability. Reportedly, a large percentage of lawsuits are the result of transporting students to and from school.
- *Homework Assignments Must Be Reasonable*: The assignment of homework is permissible, and punishment can be rendered if a student refuses to do assigned homework. However, homework should be carefully considered and reasonably assigned.

DISCUSSION QUESTIONS

1. A California case involving a student's violation of a school rule was decided in part by the fact that a school principal was not a governmental official; rather, he or she was acting in loco parentis. Give thought to the ruling of the court's view of the vice principal as a governmental official as opposed to acting as foster parent. How

might the court rule differently in each of these possible interpretations of the role of vice principal?

2. A school superintendent waived a school board ruling for a teacher regarding the amount of time a teacher could take for such occurrences as temporary illness or incapacity. The school board was sued by the teacher for not allowing the time due to extended illness toward tenure. In view of the authority of school boards and school superintendents as set forth in this chapter and others, what do you perceive as the legal ruling of the court on this matter?

3. A track coach used his own car to transport three of the team's athletes to an off-campus track meet. Three other parents drove their cars to the track meet as well. One parent, who drove one of the cars to the track meet, became ill and could not drive back home. The track coach suggested that one of the track athletes drive the car back home since he was a member of the school's driver education class. On the way back to the school, the car with the student driver ran a red light that resulted in an accident with another automobile. The student driver and another athlete who were riding in the front passenger seat were injured and had to be treated at the nearest hospital. Both the student driver and the accompanying injured athlete sued the school and track coach for damages. What information provided in chapter 3 will serve you in giving a ruling on this case?

4. Define the terms *negligence, licensee, contract, in locus parentis, de facto*, and *tort* in their legal and common law contexts. After doing so, check the glossary of legal terms at the end of the book.

5. Your science class commonly takes a field trip once each semester. Set forth the considerations that you should consider in planning this semester's trip.

6. Review the chapter section on Common Core. Do you favor/support Common Core Standards? Write a paragraph or two that sets forth your position on this matter.

CASE STUDIES

Case 3.1 It's Just a Matter of Freedom of Speech. Or Is It?

Maria Romero was a speech teacher at Wymore East Middle School. She worked with the local radio station to have her students participate in a variety of activities for the expressed purpose of gaining speaking experience. One of Romero's students, Rex Nolte, was asked to participate in a radio program that featured a round-table discussion on "Education in Our School's Today." The live radio program was impromptu in that no specific preparation was done beforehand. Rather, five or six students from the various middle schools in the district came together and talked on the topic informally.

On the evening of the radio program, the moderator asked each participant to introduce himself or herself and then commented, "Education is receiving considerable criticism today for lack of student achievement. What would each of you say about this widespread criticism? Is student achievement in schools at low ebb as we hear so often today?"

Nolte was first to respond. "I could sum up my thoughts in answer to that question in two words, lousy teachers. Teachers just don't teach anymore. I have heard that the teacher shortage is serious, but we have teachers at our school that are just incompetent. I won't mention any names, but we have students in our class that know more math than the teacher. But it isn't just in math. It is getting so that teachers do not want to teach, they just assign pages of work for us to do and hand in to them. We never see any results. The only time that our English teacher gets busy is when mandated testing times come around. Of course, few students seem to be doing well, but it's not the students' fault. If the student hasn't learned, the teacher hasn't taught."

The round-table discussion seemed to beg for closure. Other students at the table had little of significance to say but tended to shake their heads in agreement when Nolte continued with his negativity.

Question: The foregoing case, of course, is fictional but does have some similarity to the chapter cases of *Pickering v. Board of Education* and *Peter W. v. San Diego Unified School District*. If, indeed, Nolte was suspended due to his remarks on the radio program, what would the hearing officer or possibly a court want Nolte to present additionally? Is Nolte's freedom of speech protected in the case as presented? What might be your recommendation as hearing officer in this case?

Case 3.2 I Won't Do It, I Won't! My Contract States That I Will Teach Science.

Principal Simons has discussed the reading curriculum with his teachers at the high school at several of the faculty program improvement meetings during the first semester. It is his opinion that every subject matter teacher should also be a "reading teacher" as well. At the outset of the second semester, Principal Simons sends a note to each teacher requiring them to teach reading as it pertains to their particular subject. His note stresses the need for vocabulary building, reading for understanding, and reading for the purposes of extending learning in the subject field in question.

Each teacher is to receive a small amount of funding for the purchase of reading materials and resources required in the classroom. Elmira Devany, teacher of chemistry and physics, meets with Principal Simons to inform him that she cannot comply with the new reading request.

"First of all," states Mrs. Devany, "I'm not a reading teacher. I'm contracted to teach the sciences, not reading. In addition, my lab work is not conducive to teaching reading, and I do not plan to try to work such a program into an already overcrowded teaching schedule."

"It would appear to me," responds Principal Simons, "that your prime subjects give more than ample opportunities to teach the reading lessons as set forth in my note. This program is important to me and to our students. I not only expect every teacher to include reading in their daily lesson plans but am in as kind a way as I know how ordering them to do it."

"Well," says Mrs. Devany. "I think that I have the freedom to teach in my own classroom, and want you to know that I do not plan to participate in the program that you purpose."

Mrs. Devany did as she said she would do. She did not include reading in her daily lesson plans and refused to participate in the program. The school principal recommended that she be charged with insubordination and released from her position at the end of the school year.

Question: Assume the role of the hearing officer in Case 3.2. All of the information that you have is set forth in the foregoing case. Your task is to recommend follow-up actions in the case of the "I Won't Do It, I Won't!"

REFERENCES

Glink, S. E. (2015, June 24). Teacher and school staff rights: Protecting the rights of students, parents and teachers. http://www.educationrights.com/teacherrights.php.

Norton, M. S. (2008). *Human resources administration for educational leaders.* Thousand Oaks, CA: SAGE Publications, Inc.

O'Neal, C. S. (2014, August 5). *Court cases about insubordination.* Tuscaloosa, AL: University of Alabama Libraries.

Pennsylvania State Education Association. (2015, July 31). *Your speech and your job.* http://www.psea.org/teacher.aspx?id=3866.

Peterson, L. J., Rossmiller, R. A., & Volz, M. M. (1978). *The law and public school operation.* New York: Harper and Row Publishers, Inc.

Porter-Magee, K., & Stern, S. (2013, April). Why are prominent conservatives criticizing a set of rigorous educational standards? *National Review.* http://www.nationalreview.com/article/344519/truth-about-common-core-kathleen-porter-magee-sol-stern.

Pryor, B. D. (2015, June 30). Insubordination: When do you have to do as you're told . . . And when don't you? Chicago, IL: Cook County College Teachers Union, Local 1600.

Rosales, J. (2012, February 28). Fighting age discrimination against educators. *NEA Today Educational Policy: Human and Civil Rights.* National Education Association.

Sindelar, N. W. (2015, June 30). Must-read review of educators' legal responsibility & liability. Teach HUB.com. http://www.teachhub.com/educators-legal-responsibility-liability.

Tead, O., & Metcalf, H. C. (1920). *Personnel administration.* New York: McGraw-Hill.

Chapter Four

Legal Responsibilities and Liabilities in Relation to Student Personnel

Primary chapter goal: To present the legal responsibilities of school leaders in relation to their relationships with students, impact of school policies and regulations, and influence of court cases on student rights.

> The nation's highest court has had plenty to say about everything from free speech at school to teenagers' rights in the legal system.
> —Tom Jacobs, "10 Supreme Court Cases Every Teen Should Know," *New York Times*, July 21, 2015

Students are seated at their desks awaiting the opening of the school day. The tardy bell rings and the teacher asks the students to stand and recite the Pledge of Allegiance. Margo remains seated and silent during the pledge. The teacher sends Margo to the principal's office for disciplinary purposes.

In another case, Miss O'Brien, teacher of grade 6, sends a note to her principal indicating that she does not favor the principal's recent decision on "getting tough" on student retention. She points out that both empirical and basic research evidence indicate that retaining a student in a grade is more detrimental to the student's achievement than allowing the student to move to the next grade with his or her peers. She recommends that the principal's decision to retain students in a grade be withdrawn. The principal asks Miss O'Brien to meet with him after school and informs her that he is filing a personnel report on her actions for insubordination.

In a different situation, Principal Adams uses the intercom system to announce that all student lockers will be "searched" immediately after the last class period of the day. All students are to go directly to their lockers and be prepared to open them for inspection. His motive is simply a surprise strategy to check on any problems that might be discovered.

In another case, a high school senior was stopped in his car for going through a stop sign. The student was ticketed for the traffic violation and also was cited for having an illegal substance in his car. When being informed by the police of the situation, school officials suspended the student indefinitely. The student files a lawsuit on the basis that the suspension decision violated his due process rights.

At the time of this writing, a California school district was sued over its graduation dress code. The school district refused to allow a Native American student to wear an eagle feather during his high school graduation ceremony. The student claimed that his right to freedom of expression and religion in the state constitution was being violated (Thanawala, 2015, June 2).

In the first scenario concerning the Pledge of Allegiance, has the teacher acted correctly? In the second situation, when the teacher criticized the principal's decision, is the charge of insubordination appropriate? In the third situation concerning the students' locker search, has the principal acted legally? In the case of the student's indefinite suspension, what most likely will be the ruling of the court? The case of the dress code and wearing an eagle feather at graduation was undecided at the time of this writing. What are your thoughts about the outcome of this court case?

We consider the answers to the foregoing legal situations involving students and many other legal circumstances facing school leaders in this chapter of the book. First, however, we discuss the fact that school principals and other administrators are faced daily with questions relating to school policy, administrative regulations, and school rules. Unfortunately, these terms commonly are misused and not completely understood by administrators, teachers, and the school's stakeholders. We discuss many of the legal cases and federal and state legal rulings that focus on student rights and responsibilities.

Most everyone would agree that administrators and teachers should have a good knowledge of school law. Yet several studies have found that these educators commonly lack this knowledge. One study found that 60 percent of the teachers and principals could not act appropriately when having to make decisions about legal situations in public schools (Dunklee, 1985). Authorities have noted that knowledge of school law is essential since poor decisions most likely will place school personnel in court (Sorenson & Chapman, 1985; Lynch & Kuehl, 1983; Sametz et al., 1983; Ogletree & Gauett, 1981; and Peterson et al., 1978).

If administrators and teachers are to be involved in developing district policies, regulations, and school rules, it would be expected that they have clear understandings of these terms and how these terms influence their responsibilities as professionals. As noted by Bednar (1984), teachers must have a good knowledge of school law in order to do their job, meet their responsibilities, and protect the rights of students. This chapter focuses on legal court rulings that have influenced student rights relative to a variety of conditions and behaviors.

LEGAL DECISIONS RELATIVE TO LOCAL SCHOOL OPERATIONS

In the following sections of the book, the topics of student discipline, bullying, student absences, bomb threats, locker searches, dress codes, illegal substances, and other school practices are briefed. Many of the decisions relative to such matters are based on rulings of U.S. Supreme Court, state Supreme Courts, legislative statutes, and follow-up school board policies. Although the volume of court decisions and other legal decisions is much greater than can be fully discussed in this chapter, many of the most important legal decisions are considered. In addition, the brief summaries of several court cases provide an overview of each case and the rulings of the court.

Before discussing several legal rulings concerning students' rights in school, take time to answer the following ten questions. For each question posed, answer "yes" or "no." Do not just guess the answer; if you do not know the answer, move to the next question.

THE PRE-QUIZ

1. Can public school principals request drug testing for students participating in the school's extracurricular programs/activities? ____Yes or ____No
2. A minister is invited to give the invocation at the graduation exercises of the senior class of a public school. Is this a legal graduation program activity? ____Yes or ____No
3. A student reports to the school principal that another student showed him a knife that he is carrying in his backpack that is kept in his school locker. Does the principal have the right to search the student's locker? ____Yes or ____No
4. The school principal edited the school newspaper published by students and edited the lead article that he deemed inappropriate as a topic and its use of improper language. Can the principal edit the article or prohibit its publication altogether? ____Yes or ____No
5. A teacher accused a student of smoking in the bathroom. She was taken to the principal's office where the student denied the accusation of smoking. The principal searched her purse and found cigarettes and

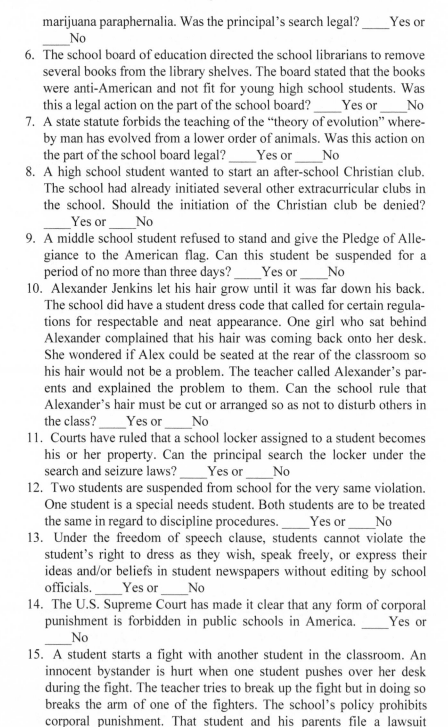

marijuana paraphernalia. Was the principal's search legal? ____Yes or ____No

6. The school board of education directed the school librarians to remove several books from the library shelves. The board stated that the books were anti-American and not fit for young high school students. Was this a legal action on the part of the school board? ____Yes or ____No

7. A state statute forbids the teaching of the "theory of evolution" whereby man has evolved from a lower order of animals. Was this action on the part of the school board legal? ____Yes or ____No

8. A high school student wanted to start an after-school Christian club. The school had already initiated several other extracurricular clubs in the school. Should the initiation of the Christian club be denied? ____Yes or ____No

9. A middle school student refused to stand and give the Pledge of Allegiance to the American flag. Can this student be suspended for a period of no more than three days? ____Yes or ____No

10. Alexander Jenkins let his hair grow until it was far down his back. The school did have a student dress code that called for certain regulations for respectable and neat appearance. One girl who sat behind Alexander complained that his hair was coming back onto her desk. She wondered if Alex could be seated at the rear of the classroom so his hair would not be a problem. The teacher called Alexander's parents and explained the problem to them. Can the school rule that Alexander's hair must be cut or arranged so as not to disturb others in the class? ____Yes or ____No

11. Courts have ruled that a school locker assigned to a student becomes his or her property. Can the principal search the locker under the search and seizure laws? ____Yes or ____No

12. Two students are suspended from school for the very same violation. One student is a special needs student. Both students are to be treated the same in regard to discipline procedures. ____Yes or ____No

13. Under the freedom of speech clause, students cannot violate the student's right to dress as they wish, speak freely, or express their ideas and/or beliefs in student newspapers without editing by school officials. ____Yes or ____No

14. The U.S. Supreme Court has made it clear that any form of corporal punishment is forbidden in public schools in America. ____Yes or ____No

15. A student starts a fight with another student in the classroom. An innocent bystander is hurt when one student pushes over her desk during the fight. The teacher tries to break up the fight but in doing so breaks the arm of one of the fighters. The school's policy prohibits corporal punishment. That student and his parents file a lawsuit

against the school and teacher. The court is highly likely to rule in favor of the parents. _____Yes or _____No

Keep your answer sheet to the foregoing questions and check them for the information given to each question as you read/study the following information set forth in the chapter. Answers: Question #1 is yes, #2 is no, #3 is yes, #4 is yes, #5 is yes, #6 is no, #7 is no, #8 is no, #9 is no, #10 is yes, #11 is yes, # 12 is no, #13 is no, #14 is no, #15 is no.

COURT CASES AND RULINGS RELATIVE TO STUDENT PERSONNEL

Case law is extremely important in its attempts to explain legal procedures concerning the rights of students and teachers. For example, it is not completely uncommon that state laws differ on rulings that seem to deal with the same or similar subjects. In many cases, the ruling depends not only on the specific conditions of the event itself but also on the nature of the student, such as if the student is disabled or not. We have found instances in which the state did not prohibit corporal punishment but a local school district did prohibit it. Does the state's position supersede that of the local school district? Even the U.S. Supreme Court has had "splits" of 5 to 4 on certain major cases, including student discipline.

Nevertheless, knowing the specific rulings by federal and state courts is of primary importance to school leaders as they complete their daily work responsibilities. The following cases illustrate court rulings that focus on the student in public school settings.

Case #1—*Tinker v. Des Moines Independent School Community* (393 U.S. 503, 1969, 1968). Freedom of Speech: Students Wore Black Armbands

Most everyone can recite the memorable words of the U.S. Supreme Court's statement relative to the fact that neither teachers nor students shed their constitutional rights to freedom of speech or expression at the schoolhouse gate. The extent to which freedom of speech is extended has since been somewhat clarified by the courts. That is, the Court has not given teachers or students the unlimited right of self-expression. The point is that self-expression must be balanced with the need to keep order and away from disrupting the work of the school and/or disturbing the rights of others.

The specific case that fostered the Supreme Court's actions was based on a case whereby students wore black armbands to school to protest the war activities in Vietnam. When the students refused to remove their armbands, they were suspended. The students and their parents brought a lawsuit against the school district on the basis of their freedom of speech rights under the First Amendment of the U.S. Constitution. The Court decided in favor of the students since their actions did not disrupt classroom work, cause disorder with other school activities, or invade the rights of others. The significance of the Supreme Court's ruling underscored the fact that the U.S. Constitution does not permit school personnel to deny students the right to this kind of expression.

Case #2 — *Broussard v. School Board of Norfolk* (802 F. Supp. 1526, E. D. Va. (1992)). Freedom of Speech

A student wore a T-shirt to school that had the words "Drugs Suck" on it. As a result, he was disciplined for wearing the shirt. He filed a lawsuit claiming that his First Amendment rights had been violated. The court disagreed and ruled in favor of the school board. The shirt message was not allowed in schools since it was vulgar and carried with it a sexual connotation.

Case #3 — *Morse v. Frederick* (551 U.S., 127 S. Ct. 2618, 2007). Freedom of Speech and Its Intent

A senior student in a high school in Juneau, Alaska, was attending the school activity of the Olympic Torch Relay. He had a banner that had the words, "Bong Hits 4 Jesus." The school principal asked Joseph Frederick to put the banner away. Frederick refused to comply with the principal's request, so she took the banner away from him. She had concerns that the statement on the banner would be interpreted as supporting illegal drug activity. Frederick was given a ten-day suspension for violating school drug policy.

The District of Alaska's U.S. District Court supported the principal and stated that the First Amendment did not protect Frederick's actions. The Appeals Court of the Ninth District heard the case, and that court reversed the previous ruling, indicating that the First Amendment protected Frederick's banner. The U.S. Supreme Court granted certiorari whereby a writ seeking judicial review was ordered.

The Supreme Court ruled that the statement "Bong Hits 4 Jesus" could indeed be interpreted as promoting illegal drugs. Did the principal violate the student's rights to free speech when the speech is reasonably viewed as promoting illegal drug use? Although not a unanimous ruling, the U.S. Supreme Court ruled no.

Case #4 — *Desilets v. Clearview Regional Board of Education* (137 N.J. 585; 647 A.2d 150; 1994 N.J. LEXIS 844 (N.J. 1994))

Brien Desilets was a seventh-grade student at Clearview Junior High School. He became involved with the school newspaper and wrote reviews on two R-rated films for publication in the newspaper. The school principal prohibited the publishing of the articles since the films were R rated. An article from the Web (School of Journalism and Communication, 2015, July 22) contained the following review by the student, Brien Desilets:

> *Rain Man,* Rated R (Starring Tom Cruise and Dustin Hoffman)
> In this film, Charlie Babbitt (Tom Cruise) finds that he has a brother, Raymond (Dustin Hoffman) that [*sic*] has inherited three million dollars in their father's will. However, Raymond is autistic and does not [*sic*] understood the concept of money. Charlie then kidnaps "Rain Man" from the mental institution, and the two leave for a weeklong drive across the country. On this ride the two become great friends and experience many adventures. Dustin Hoffman did an excellent job of playing an autistic savant. The movie is hilariously funny and I think that everyone should see it.

Brien filed a lawsuit claiming that his First Amendment rights had been violated and that New Jersey's free press clause had been violated as well. The court ruled that the student's rights were violated under the state's constitution but not the U.S. Constitution. An Appellate Division ruled that Brien's rights had been violated under the First Amendment of the federal Constitution, and the New Jersey State Supreme Court agreed.

The crux of the case centers on the precedent that school officials must have a legitimate educational justification for censoring nonforum student newspapers. Such decisions based on personal opinions or ones not clearly stated in policy are not viable for behaviors related to censorship. That is, a clearly stated school policy looms important in censorship decisions regarding freedom of speech in school newspapers.

Follow-up court decisions relative to dress codes, student newspapers, and vulgar and/or inappropriate language have implemented the "disruptive clause" to rule on many other cases of student behavior; for example, the courts have ruled unfavorably on certain cases that involved student speeches that included sexual implications or the wearing of T-shirts with vulgar or other inappropriate language. In a recent case, for example, the Supreme Court ruled in favor of limiting student speech if it tended to suggest/advocate the illegal use of drugs.

Other freedom of speech cases have centered on "what students have said," "how it was said," and "where they have said it."

Case #5—*New Jersey v. TLO* (469 U.S. 325, 1985). Privacy Rights at School

This case holds many implications for search and seizure of students' property on their person, in lockers, and in personal possessions. T.L.O. was a young, female high school student in New Jersey. A teacher found her smoking in the girls' bathroom. The principal of the school asked to see her purse. After finding cigarettes and marijuana in the purse, the principal called the police. According to the police, the girl admitted selling drugs at school.

The girl was placed on probation after being found guilty in court of possession of marijuana. T.L.O. appealed the court's decision, saying that her Fourth Amendment rights of unreasonable searches and seizures were violated. The Supreme Court ruled that the search did not violate the Fourth Amendment since the evidence of the case revealed that such a search was reasonable under the circumstances. The evidence in the purse justified further searching. The principal showed reasonableness in searching the purse, and the evidence used against the girl in this case was properly gathered.

Case #6—*Merrikan et al. v. Cressman et al.* (United States District Court, E. D. Pennsylvania, September 28, 1973). Matter of Student Privacy

This case is interesting in that it underscores the fact that students in a school setting do not have the full protection of privacy that is enjoyed by adults. In this case, a school district in Pennsylvania wanted to identify drug abusers. Questions centered on parent-child relationships and practices of parents. It was administered without the permission of parents. The case was important since it established the right of parents to be free from an invasion of their privacy. The court, however, did not address the privacy rights of students in a school setting.

Other related court cases are noteworthy as well. In the case of *Sterling v. Borough of Minersville* (2000), the ruling of the court suggested that principals and all other school personnel should refrain from giving information to others about a student's sexual orientation without the student's, and we expect the parents', permission. Other cases have underscored the importance of principals, school psychologists, and other school personnel not gathering or storing private information about any personnel (i.e., students, teachers, parents, etc.) that cannot be justified as needed in implementing the educational services provided by the school.

We discuss later the case of *New Jersey v. T.L.O.* (1985), where the Supreme Court indicated that the Fourth Amendment of the Constitution protected student rights from unreasonable search and seizure in public schools. In this case, the "reasonable suspicion" standard was upheld. Although the nature of the suspicion must be more than a guess or rumor, if school officials have reasonable grounds to suspect that a search will indeed produce evidence that a violation was committed, the courts tend to give full support to school locker or personal searches.

The outcome for school principals and others centers on the ruling that "suspicion based" searches are permissible. If the schoolteacher or administrator has reasonable suspicion that a school rule is violated or a crime is likely to be committed, a reasonable search of a student's property is permissible.

Case #7—*Ingraham v. Wright* (430 U.S. 651, 1977). School Discipline and Corporal Punishment. State of Florida

Court cases on corporal punishment are problematic in that approximately one-half of the states permit schools to use corporal punishment and one-half do not. The actual percentages indicate that approximately six more states prohibit the practice than the number of states that permit it. The matter of corporal punishment has been left to the individual states. The wise advice regarding corporal punishment even if approved by the state is to be cautious about when and how the punishment is administered.

In the case at hand, James Ingraham, a young junior high school student, was taken to the school principal's office after a teacher indicated he had become unruly in the school auditorium. The principal decided to give the student a few swats with a paddle. The student insisted that he had not misbehaved and refused to be paddled. Instead of administering the few swats, the student was held down and given twenty swats with the paddle.

Florida did not have a ruling against corporal punishment. The student and his mother filed a lawsuit against the school principals and others based on their claim that the Eighth Amendment protected James from cruel and unusual punishment. James reportedly did receive bruises that kept him from school, and he also had to obtain medical services.

Nevertheless, the Supreme Court ruled that reasonable corporal punishment did not violate the Constitution; that is, the Eighth Amendment was meant for criminals and not for implementation in the school setting. In addition, the Court held that the Fourteenth Amendment relative to due process did not apply to corporal punishment since it was imposed negatively on the area of educational authority. The underlying learning point in this case is that caution should be used in every case of corporal punishment and that the case at hand be given serious consideration relative to its seriousness, past student's behavior record, and the student's attitude, age, and physical condition. In addition, other methods of discipline should be considered in cases of student misbehavior.

Case #8—*Hazelwood School District v. Kuhlmeier et al.* (484 U.S. 260, 1988). Student Journalism and the First Amendment, St. Louis, Missouri

This case centers on the ability of school personnel to censor student newspapers. Three high school students, who were members of the journalism class and served as writers and editors of the school paper, wrote an article on the topic of parental divorce and its impact on student pregnancy. The proposed article was rejected by the school principal on the basis that it was not appropriate for younger students and also contained inappropriate personal details. On the basis that their First Amendment rights of freedom of speech were being violated, the girls took the case to court.

The court ruled in favor of the school district, stating that a school newspaper is not to be used as a public forum; rather, it is a learning experience for students relative to journalism. That is, the school has a responsibility for supervising and controlling the style and content of student speech in all of the various student activities. The First Amendment is not violated when school personnel exercise control over related speech activities as long as their actions are reasonable and center on legitimate educational perspectives. In doing so, the court cautioned that school personnel should use caution in censoring student speech by seeking a balance between speech standards and recognizing students' rights to freedom of speech.

Case #9—*Westside Community Schools v. Mergens* (496 U.S. 226, 1990). Student Clubs in the School—Religious Clubs

A senior high school student at Westside High School in Omaha, Nebraska, asked permission to initiate an after-school Christian club. The school principal denied the request, stating that such a club would not be legal in a public school. The high school already had several student clubs associated with the school, and Congress had recently passed legislation (Equal Access Act, 1984) that allowed schools to permit religious clubs if other student interest clubs already were in existence.

A lawsuit filed by the student ultimately became the test case for deciding the legality of the Equal Access Act. The Supreme Court acted in order to decide if the Equal Access Act was constitutional under the Establishment Clause of the First Amendment, whereby "Congress shall make no law respecting an establishment of religion, or prohibiting the free exercise thereof."

The Supreme Court ruled in favor of the Westside High School student and stated that allowing students to meet on campus after school to discuss religion did not amount to state sponsorship of religion. Since the school had previously approved several clubs that were not related to educational goals and objectives of the school, it could not exclude clubs that center on religion, politics, or other such topics.

In summary, teachers are permitted to sponsor religious clubs. Some differences depend on whether the religious club meets during the regular school day or meets after school hours. If outside the regular school hours and other types of extracurricular clubs have been approved for students, the religious club could be led by an adult or by a schoolteacher. However, in these cases, the teacher must be acting as a private citizen as opposed to a teacher who is sponsoring the club. Such religious clubs held during school hours appear to be permitted if the club is student initiated and student led. The actual teaching of religion in the school curriculum has not been considered as a violation of the First Amendment if indeed it is relevant to the school curriculum. As stated by Staver (2005): "The more relevant the information to the curriculum, the stronger the constitutional protection" (p. 19).

Case #10—*Engel v. Vitale* (370 U.S. 421, 1962). Praying in the Schools

A parent in New Hyde Park Island sued the public schools claiming that a prayer recommended by the New York State Board of Regents for students to say in their schools was forbidden by the First Amendment of the U.S. Constitution. The school argued that the prayer was nondenominational; it was not required and it did not in any way endorse a religion in the school. The Supreme Court ruled in favor of the parent and indicated that schools could not sponsor such religious activities. Prayer for students initiated by the school violates the First Amendment.

Case #11—*Goss v. Lopez* (419 U.S., 565 U.S., 1976). Students and Due Process of Law

A group of nine students including D. Lopez were suspended from school for unacceptable conduct and was not afforded a hearing or any procedures of due process. School officials were under the impression that a student could be suspended for ten days without due process protection. The students brought legal action claiming that their Fourth Amendment rights had been abridged. The argument centered on whether or not the school should suspend a student for ten days without implementing due process procedures. The U.S. Supreme Court ruled that suspending a student without the opportunity for a hearing did indeed violate the student's rights under the Fourteenth Amendment. Due process procedures are required, including prior notice when suspension is given for more than a trivial time period. If the student denies the charges, a hearing is required. The procedures for implementing such a hearing are set forth later in the chapter.

Case #12—*Plessey v. Ferguson* (163 U.S. 537, 1896). Civil Rights and Segregation

In this early court case, Plessey argued that Blacks were not being given equal rights under the Fourteenth Amendment since they had to ride in separate train cars. Plessey had been arrested for violating the law in this regard. The state was of the opinion that Blacks were being given equal treatment, although it included separation. The Court agreed with the state and the concept of "separate but equal" was accepted for fifty-eight years until *Brown v. the Board of Education* (Topeka, Kansas) reversed the *Plessey* decision, stating that separate schools are inherently unequal.

Case #13—*Brown v Board of Education* (341k7 U.S. 483, 1952) (Topeka, Kansas). Civil Rights and Segregation

Although there was a White school just across the street from Linda Brown's home, she had to walk five miles to attend her school for Blacks. The head of the NAACP, Thurgood Marshall, took the case to the court, claiming that segregation laws violated the Fourteenth Amendment of the U.S. Constitution. Students were to receive equal treatment under the law. The state argued that the *Plessey v. Ferguson* case had settled this question and that separate but equal was being practiced. The court under Justice Earl Warren ruled in favor of the Brown family, and the initiation of integration was installed as the legal practice in America.

Case #14—*Board of Education of Independent School District #92 of Pottawatomie County v. Earls* (536 U.S. 822, 2002). Random Drug Testing of Students

The Supreme Court upheld the right of random drug testing for students who were involved in athletics. Such testing did not violate the Fourth Amendment's clause that prohibits unreasonable search and seizure. In later actions, the Court upheld drug tests for all students in extracurricular activities.

Case #15—*Vernonia School District v. Acton* (515 U.S. 646, 1995). Drug Testing for Students Participating in Athletics

The school required drug testing for all students participating in sports activities. A young student, twelve years of age, wanted to participate in the football program, but the student's parents refused to allow him to be tested for drugs. His parents claimed that mandatory drug testing was prohibited by the Fourteenth Amendment without suspicion of illegal drug use. The Supreme Court ruled in favor of the school district, noting that (1) it was important for schools to keep athletes away from drugs, (2) students do give up some privacy rights while at school and athletes give up even more than others, (3) participating in athletics usually requires giving up some privacy rights relative to physical examinations, showering, changing in locker rooms, and other such necessities. Later court cases have ruled in favor of drug testing for students participating in all extracurricular activities in public schools.

Case #16—*Epperson v. Arkansas* (393 U.S. 97, 1968). Teaching the Theory of Evolution in Public Schools

A teacher in Arkansas was fired for violating a state law that prohibited the teaching of the theory that man evolved from a lower order of animals. The Supreme Court of the United States reviewed the case relative to the question of whether or not the teaching of the theory violated the Establishment Clause of the First Amendment and the Equal Protection Clause of the Fourteenth Amendment. The Court ruled that the Arkansas statute forbidding the teaching of evolution violated the freedom of religion clause in the First Amendment and also violated the Fourteenth Amendment concerning freedom of religion; that is, the state cannot control/eliminate courses from the school curriculum just because they do not agree with ideas of various religious groups in the school community. Since the purpose of the group that supported the removing of the present statute was to support a specific religious view, it was an abridgement of the First Amendment.

Case #17—*Lee v. Weisman* (505 U.S. 577, 1992). Religious Ceremonies at Student Graduations

This case centered on whether or not schools are permitted to have certain religious exercises at graduation ceremonies such as benedictions and invocations. Lee was a principal of a middle school in Rhode Island, and Weisman was the father of the middle school student, Deborah Weisman.

Principal Lee had invited a rabbi to give prayers for Deborah Weisman's class graduation. As a result, Deborah's father asked for a restraining order to prohibit the school from having such prayers at the graduation, but the District Court denied the motion to restrain the prayers at the ceremony.

After the ceremony, Weisman requested a permanent injunction for stopping further practices of inviting clergy to deliver benedictions and invocations at future graduation ceremonies of the school district. The focus was that of deciding whether prayers given by clergy at graduation ceremonies violated the Establishment Clause of the First Amendment. The court ruled yes. Such involvement by clergy in the graduation ceremonies did carry the possibility of coercing students to support or participate in religion or serve in a manner that establishes religion or religious faith.

Although Principal Lee had informed the rabbi of the fact that his remarks had to be nondenominational, this fact alone tended to direct and control the prayer's content. Thus, the state cannot put the student who is dissenting in the position of involvement or having to protest. In addition, the argument that a student does not have to attend the graduation ceremonies is not acceptable. In reality, it has been pointed out that a student is not really free to be absent from graduation ceremonies. To place him or her in the position of being absent or attending graduation ceremonies is asking for the student to decide whether to miss one of life's most memorable experiences or to submit to a government-sponsored program; this brings about a high conflict of conscience (Hardin, 2015).

Case #18—*T.K. and S.K. v. New York City Department of Education* (10-cv-00752 [E.D.N.Y. April 20, 2011] [8]). Bullying

A handicapped student filed a claim with a New York federal district court stating that she had been denied a free and appropriate education under the federal Individuals with Disabilities Education Act (IDEA). The claim was based on "bullying" received from peers due to her disability and the fact that the school leaders had not curtailed the bullying that was taking place. A general "ruling" resulted from the court that schools should take the responsibility of acting promptly to stop bullying due to the fact that it could interfere with a student's ability to gain an appropriate education.

Case #19—*Honig v. Doe* (484 U.S. 305, 1988). Emotionally Disturbed Children and the Stay Put Provision of EHA/IDEA

Two emotionally disturbed children were suspended after destroying school property and abusing other children at the school. An indefinite suspension was initiated while the school officials were preparing for further action. The students brought a lawsuit and contended that the stay put provision of the EHA/IDEA Act was being abridged. They contested that a new placement provision could not be implemented while proceedings for a change in placement was being considered. In fact, a new Individual Education Plan had to be approved before a placement change could be implemented.

The Court ruled that a change in placement had indeed occurred and this violated the Education for All Handicapped Children Act. The Court did agree that the school officials could temporarily suspend the students for the ten-day period. In this way, the school could act to protect the safety of others, could review the IEP and convince others that it needed to be changed, and could seek court rulings regarding the exclusion of students that endangered the lives of others. As a result, two facts were important in the Court's rulings. One, suspension for ten days was permissible in such cases and did not constitute a change in the student's placement, and two, when the behavior of a student is related to his or her disability, expulsion from school would not be approved.

Case #20—*Santa Fe Independent School District v. Doe* (s530 U.S. 290, 2000). Use of School Property to Offer Student–Led Prayer

Students at a high school in Texas selected a classmate to "address" the football team and those in attendance at football games over a loudspeaker owned by the school. The address took place before football games and commonly included a prayer. The practice was opposed by two sets of former and current students and their mothers, and they sued on the basis that such a prayer violated the Establishment Clause of Amendment I. School officials based their case on their opinion that the prayer was student initiated and not sponsored by the school. Other courts acted on this matter before it came to the U.S. Supreme Court for final ruling. A majority of the U.S. Supreme Court ruled against the school officials, indicating that the activity was a school-sponsored prayer since the speakers used by the students was school property. As stated by majority opinion: It is held that these pregame prayers delivered "on the property, at school-sponsored events, over the school's public address system, by a speaker representing the student body, under the supervision of school faculty, and pursuant to a school policy that explicitly and implicitly encourages public prayer," are not private but public speech.

A dissenting opinion was written by the Chief Justice of the Court, Justice Rehnquist, and argued that in fact the district's policy on this matter had yet to be put into practice. In addition, the address/speech in question was to be private and chosen and delivered by the speaker, as opposed to a public-school-sponsored address (Wikipedia, June 19, 2015, p. 1).

Case #21—*Bethel School District No. 403 v. Fraser* (478 U.S. 675, 1986). Lewd Speeches by Students at the School

A high school student at Bethel High School participated in what was viewed as obscene and lewd speech at a school assembly program. The speech included sexual metaphors that in some way were to promote the election to office of a fellow classmate. School officials were of the opinion that the speech violated the school's conduct code and served to interfere with the educational process of the school. The student was suspended for two days following the assembly speech. Fraser, the student, sued on the basis that the school violated his First Amendment rights of freedom of speech. Members of the U.S. Supreme Court ruled in favor of the school officials, stating that it was not appropriate for students to use vulgar and offensive language in the school. Such discourse is inconsistent with the fundamental values of public education.

A POSITIVE LOOK AT CORPORAL PUNISHMENT

Earlier in the chapter, the topic of corporal punishment was discussed in relation to the U.S. Supreme Court case of *Ingraham v. Wright*. In that case, the Court found that students could be paddled without first receiving a hearing. The ruling was based on a 5 to 4 decision. In brief, the majority voiced the opinion that the Eighth Amendment of the U.S. Constitution only referred to convicted criminals and the ban on cruel and unusual punishment did not apply to noncriminals. Furthermore, rulings to change a new ruling held the risk of violating student rights and also tended to interfere in an area that was primarily a responsibility of education.

One justice noted that a school disciplinarian could give a student notice of the charges forthrightly, permit the student to give an explanation of the evidence in hand, and then give the student an opportunity to present his or her side of the matter.

Local school policies and state statutes tend to differ on the question of corporal punishment for students. The Wake County Public School System, for example, cites its board policy on corporal punishment as follows:

6525 Corporal Punishment

Believing that other forms of discipline are more appropriate with children of all ages, the Wake County Board of Education prohibits the use of corporal punishment. No principal, assistant principal, teacher, substitute teacher, any other school system employee or volunteer may use corporal punishment to discipline any student.

On the other hand, the U.S. Supreme Court has given schools "substantial constitutional leeway" in carrying out their responsibilities for responding to wrongdoing on the part of students. It is quite obvious that school districts need to develop a policy that does not conflict with any student discipline statutes of the state and encompasses the cultural opinions of the school community. In any case, we submit that a positive approach to student discipline will realize the best results. "Proactive school-wide discipline systems create environments in which learning and teaching are valued, aggressive and unsafe behavior are discouraged and respect, responsibility, cooperation and other highly valued traits are taught and encouraged" (Mississippi Department of Education, 2006, p. 31). The Department's statement included seven procedures for developing a schoolwide system for student discipline:

1. Behavior Expectations Are Defined—Positive rules are expected.

2. Behavior Expectations Are Taught—Opportunity to practice the right way.
3. Appropriate Behaviors Are Acknowledged—Positive behavior is rewarded.
4. Behavior Errors Are Corrected Proactively—Clear procedures for unacceptable behavior.
5. Program Evaluations and Adaptations Are Made by a Team—Assessments for measuring program success are ongoing.
6. Administrative Support and Involvement Are Active—Schoolwide administrator support is in evidence.
7. Individual Student Support Systems Are Integrated with Schoolwide Discipline Systems—The discipline process focuses on developing a positive discipline culture/climate in the school. Successful programs implement policies and procedures that support both academic and social/behavioral success and results in positive student success.

A FURTHER LOOK AT STUDENT DISCIPLINE

Data from the principal survey reported in chapter 2 revealed that approximately 85 percent of the respondents viewed student discipline as a serious or difficult legal problem facing them. In regard to student discipline, what is the authority of teachers to exercise authority over the students in his or her classroom? Is the concept of in loco parentis accepted as a legal practice in schools? What is meant by *procedural due process*, and how is it different from *substantive due process*? How does detention differ from suspension? How does suspension differ from expulsion? Can the school discipline a student for an act committed off school grounds? Can the school control students at home? We consider the legal answers to these questions in the following section of the chapter.

Detention is the holding of a student when he or she is free to go home, attend recess, or to participate in after-school intermural sports. This form of "punishment" commonly is used in cases of less serious cases of student violations of school rules. When the detention is used reasonably and for good reason, there is little cause for concern that detention will not be ruled permissible through a hearing or by a court. If the act of the student has a negative effect on the conduct requirements of the school, it makes no difference if the violation took place on or outside the school grounds. From a legal point of view, the act itself, not the site of the act, is what determines the school's right to implement punishment on the violator. The legal perspective historically has been that suspension or expulsion can be implemented when a student refuses to obey a reasonable rule that has been communicated to the student body.

Student suspension is viewed legally as a stopping of a student's right that most often comes as an exclusion from attending school. In most cases, suspension is limited to no more than three days, and if no further action is necessary, the student can return to school. However, courts have ruled that any suspension that requires an indefinite period of time or more than three days does require the implementation of due process procedures. It is common practice to have the legal procedures for student suspension set forth in a state's statutes. In such cases, a school district often includes the statute in its policy manual verbatim. The action is taken to reduce the chances of having a lawsuit dismissed on the basis that it did not follow the procedures required in the state statute on suspension.

Expulsion is viewed as taking away the rights of an individual to be a member of a body or society for a violation that results in the person losing his or her rights to membership. Due process procedures commonly accompany expulsion cases whereby a student hearing is conducted. Unless approval is set forth in the statutes of the state, the professional staff cannot expel a student. Expulsion is left to the decision of the school's Board of Education.

Several court cases have underscored certain guidelines for student expulsion. For example, a student can be expelled from school for not having a valid excuse when absences and tardiness become excessive. A student cannot be expelled due to his or her low school achievement or the fact that he or she is just difficult to teach. Another important point centers on the ruling that an expulsion cannot last beyond the current year. A student that has been expelled cannot be refused attendance at public entertainment programs held at the school when all members of the public are invited to attend. If a student who was expelled from a school transfers to another school, he or she cannot be expelled for the same reason at the new school. A student cannot be expelled due to the belief that he or she might disrupt education unless there is strong evidence to substantiate that feat (Peterson et al., 1978).

Sexual Harassment

Studies have revealed that a high percentage of students have received unwanted and unwelcomed behavior of a sexual nature (Stein, 2013). Sexual conduct was considered as a serious or difficult problem facing 84.5 percent of school principals who participated in the legal survey reported in chapter 2. Sexual harassment comes in a variety of inappropriate behaviors, including sexual comments, jokes, gestures, or looks to actual touching or grabbing in a sexual way. Unlawful sexual harassment can occur when a school employee sets certain conditions for some educational decisions on the submission of some form of sexual favors on the part of the student, or if a student is threatened by another student if they do not submit to some sexual activity.

The case of *Davis v. Monroe County Board of Education* (No. 97-843) involved a fifth-grade girl that was sexually taunted by a classmate. Despite numerous complaints from the female student and her mother, school officials did not take action to stop the harassment. The parents used Title IX and the right of students to have access to the educational opportunities and benefits of a quality education. The Supreme Court ruled that school districts can be held liable for damages under federal law in student-to-student sexual harassment cases when harassment is "severe and pervasive" and the school knows about the harassment and fails to do something about it.

Sexuality and Student Rights and Privacy Considerations

Matters of sexuality among students have become a subject of primary concern. Gender identity and transgender issues loom large among the sexuality issues that are encountered by school principals in schools nationally. Maintaining a safe and educational environment that is free from bullying and discrimination because of a student's gender identity centers on a variety of administrative matters. Privacy and the confidentiality of student information, use of facilities such as restrooms and locker room accessibility, gender segregation in other school activities, participation in sports and physical education activities, in school student relationships, dress codes, gender designation changes, and other relationships have become administrative matters for practicing school principals at all school levels. Privacy in these matters is of utmost importance. As noted by the adopted school policy of the Mesa Public Schools, disclosing student information to other employees, students, parents, or other third parties may violate privacy laws, including, but not limited to, FERPA (Family Educational Rights and Privacy Act).

The U.S. Supreme Court or district courts have not ruled specifically on these matters, although FERPA has set forth student rights relative to several of these issues/problems. Fair and equal treatment has been the "rulings" on sexuality matters. Parental custodianship has loomed significantly as a legal matter as well. A student's legal name has also become a legal matter for which principals must contend. This is why many school districts have adopted a policy relative to legal name changes on the part of students. For example, the Mesa Public Schools in Mesa, Arizona, have adopted an official school policy that is briefly stated in the following section.

> It is the policy of Mesa Public Schools (MPS) to maintain a safe and supportive learning and educational environment that is free from harassment, bullying, and discrimination because of a student's gender identity. . . . Disclosing confidential student information to other employees, students, parents, and other third parties may violate privacy laws, including but not limited to FERPA.

Mesa Public Schools must maintain for each enrolled student an official student record that includes the student's legal name. The student's legal name must be used in all legal records, including a transcript, high school diploma, and reports to the Arizona Department of Education. A student's legal name will be changed by the Mesa Public Schools in its official student records upon receipt of official documentation required that the name has been changed pursuant to applicable law. (School Board Policy, Mesa Public Schools, Mesa, Arizona. Used by permission)

Cyberbullying: A Growing Problem

Cyberbullying includes inappropriate, harassing, and embarrassing photos and statements sent to individuals using technical equipment such as cell phones, computers, and a variety of other communication tools. Its intent is to "hurt" other people and commonly results in prohibiting the learning process for the person being bullied. Empirical evidence suggests that students being bullied can suffer a decrease in learning achievement, a loss of self-esteem, increased school absenteeism, more health problems, and serious depression.

Authorities argue that cyberbullying is different in that it can take place any time of the day or night and is difficult or even impossible to trace. A bullying message can be quickly sent to a wide audience and is difficult to delete (U.S. Department of Health & Human Services, 2015). School leaders view cyberbullying as being different than in-school bullying, and thus it presents many new challenges. Recall that the principal survey reported in chapter 2 revealed that cyberbullying was viewed by 55.4 percent of school principals as one of the most serious problems facing them.

Webwise (2015, August 5) recommends several things that school leaders can do to battle against online bullying. The recommendations include:

- *Support*—Provide the person being bullied with support and reassurance. Ensure them that there is support there for them.
- *Evidence*—Help the child keep relevant evidence for investigation. Do not allow the deletion of phone messages.
- *Inform*—Give the child advice for making sure it does not happen again (e.g., changing passwords, contact details, and blocking profiles on social networking sites).
- *No Retaliation*—Ensure that the young person does not retaliate or reply to the messages.
- *Privacy*—Encourage the child to keep personal information private on the Internet.
- *Investigation*—The cyberbullying claim needs to be investigated fully.
- *Report*—Abuse on social networking sites needs to be reported to the website and phone service providers.

- *Guidelines*—Your school will have (or must have) a number of policy documents that you can refer to, including antibullying and disciplinary policies. (p. 2)

Webwise (2015, August 5) further suggests that the best way to prevent cyberbullying is to treat it as a school community issue as well as viewing it as being different from bullying within the current school's antibullying policy. Placing an emphasis on developing a positive school climate has been recommended as a positive solution to a number of major issues facing school leaders, including student academic performance, student-to-student relationships, student absenteeism, and personal student self-esteem (Norton, 2015). Webwise (2015) points out that preventing cyberbullying will not be easy since it is difficult to police. Nevertheless, the following preventative measures were recommended:

1. Treat cyberbullying as a school community issue.
2. Make certain that students understand that all bullying is wrong and will not be tolerated.
3. Teach students their rights and responsibilities about online use.
4. Promote the positive use of technology, good etiquette, and personal safety issues.
5. Make sure that students understand the ways of reporting cyberbullying.
6. Keep antibullying policies and regulations constantly updated.
7. Encourage a supportive and positive atmosphere in the school that assures that cyberbullying will not thrive.

Although court cases remain somewhat limited on matters such as schools and transgender students, a significant court case in Virginia is of special interest. This case, reported in a Gust Rosenfeld Client Alert of October 2015, is reported briefly herein.

Title IX, Schools and Transgender Students, G.C. v. Gloucester County Schools. The U.S. District Court for the Eastern District of Virginia recently issued a decision in the emerging area of Title IX requirements with respect to transgender students. The plaintiff, a transgender student, filed suit under Title IX and the Equal Protection Clause alleging that the Gloucester County School Board's resolution limiting bathrooms and locker rooms to students and others of the corresponding sex was unlawful.

The court granted the district's motion to dismiss the complaint, relying heavily on Title IX regulation that permits separate toilet, locker room, and shower facilities on the basis of sex so long as they are comparable (34 C.F.R. 106.33). The court also rejected the "Statement of Interest" of the U.S. Department of Education (USDOE) specifically stating that USDOE's recent interpretation in opinion letters and published guidance on a transgender student's access to such facilities are "plainly erroneous and inconsistent with [34 CFR 106.33]."

DUE PROCESS AND THE DISCIPLINARY HEARING PROCEDURES

The underlying purpose of a student disciplinary hearing is that of fairness. When the possibility of suspension or expulsion is probable, the due process procedure is in order. It is of paramount importance that the student is notified of specific violation(s) and the right to respond to the charges. In some cases, the nature of the violation is such that an informal hearing is held that includes the student, parents or guardian, and the teacher or administrator of the school.

During *informal hearings*, the violation charges are presented/clarified and the "penalties" are identified. The student is granted the opportunity to respond to the charges and to explain his or her views as to what happened in the case at hand. In many instances, those in attendance are able to reach an agreement as to the follow-up of the charges and the possible ways in which the case can be resolved. If certain "penalties" are agreed upon, they are enforced at the school building level and the case is closed when they have been attended. In many instances, the informal hearing alone serves to resolve the problem at hand; that is, the student shows that a lesson has been learned and confidence in a positive behavior hereafter can be expected.

A *formal* disciplinary *hearing* commonly is held when a student is facing suspension, expulsion, or other reprimands for more than ten school days. Procedures for student hearing, if not set forth in state statutes, are determined by school board policy. Perhaps the most formal arrangement is when the formal hearing is conducted by a Disciplinary Hearing Authority that commonly consists of members appointed by the school board, whereby a specified number are licensed employees of the school board.

More commonly perhaps, a hearing officer is appointed by the school board, school superintendent, or school principal to appoint a qualified neutral person to conduct the hearing. The hearing "agenda" usually includes an orientation as to how the hearing will be conducted, a notice of the charges given by the school principal or other appropriate school member, an opportunity for the student to present his or her story and to rebut the charges, the presence of witnesses on behalf of the accused student, the right of the accused to speak on his or her behalf, and the right to cross-examine witnesses. Whether or not the student can have an attorney present depends on the state statutes or common agreement between the two parties. Unless the state statutes or the school board policies specify otherwise, student hearings are closed in that only the hearing officer, school principal or his or her representative, student, parents or guardians, and counsel if approved are present. Witnesses that participate in the hearing are present only at the time they are testifying. Keep in mind that a witness can be requested to testify but is not legally required to do so.

The hearing officer controls/conducts the hearing and takes all steps necessary to retain fairness in the proceedings. The hearing officer opens the hearing by giving a brief clarification of the hearing process and setting forth the procedures that will be followed. The officer commonly answers any questions posed concerning the hearing procedures.

The hearing officer does not act as a judge in these cases. Rather, the hearing officer serves to make certain that all parties are notified of the time, place, and date for the hearing; completes the procedural agenda for the meeting; and keeps accurate minutes of the hearing and submits the minutes to the school superintendent/director as specified by the school board. The hearing officer's report is expected to include the facts presented in the hearing by both the student and the school representative. The superintendent's report to the school board commonly includes a recommendation for or against suspension or expulsion. However, only the school board can expel a student from school unless specified differently in the state's statutes.

THE ROLE OF THE SCHOOL PRINCIPAL IN STUDENT SUSPENSION AND EXPULSION

Suspending or recommending expulsion is one of the most difficult actions/ decision that a school principal must make. Approximately 38 percent of the school principals in the aforementioned legal survey viewed student sexual conduct as a serious problem being encountered. Principals who are student advocates make use of every effort to resolve a student problem before the need for a hearing is determined. Face-to-face meetings with the student and with his parents are common, and interventions such as on-campus detention or other staff interventions are considered before recommending a student hearing (Norton, Kelly, & Battle, 2012).

When a hearing is recommended, the school principal must take full responsibility for seeing that when the hearing is held that the information presented by the school is accurate, documented, and fairly reported. Has the student been treated fairly in the matter to date? Have the student's rights been protected? Has the student received competent counsel? Have the student's parents/guardians been properly informed of the violation and its probable consequences? Have the state's statutes and the school board's policies been accurately followed in the matter to date, and will they be followed in case a hearing does occur?

As summarized by Norton and others (2012):

> The school principal who recommends that a student be subjected to a suspension or expulsion has exhausted all the resources at his or her disposal in order to help the student make better decisions relative to future behavior. Committing to advocating for students in disciplinary cases will minimize the need to recommend students for serious punishment; other alternatives are more likely to result in positive learning for the student and support rather than inhibit future positive behavior. (p. 90)

In summary, it is somewhat difficult to set forth "absolute" laws in regard to student suspension and expulsion. That is, the varied outcomes of court cases, differences in state statutes, and differences in school board policies are prevalent. As previously noted in this chapter, even the U.S. Supreme Court was divided on the issue of corporal punishment. Nevertheless, wise advice tends to indicate that a court hearing is required in all cases of nonemergency student suspensions. In addition, it appears to be established that a student can be suspended or expelled for refusing to comply with a reasonable school rule. To be safe in making decisions on student discipline matters, it always is best to be knowledgeable of state statutes, school board policies, and the school's own rules on student discipline cases. Not doing so certainly will result in losing a matter at any government or court level.

FEDERAL LEGISLATION AND COURT RULINGS REGARDING SPECIAL NEEDS STUDENTS

A majority of the school principals questioned in one case did not know that principals are required by law to find all children with special needs in their school districts. The search and find law is required even though a disabled child may not be a potential enrollee in the principal's school (Norton et al., 2012). Although there have been many court cases concerning the rights of students with special needs, three federal laws have set forth the primary requirement for serving handicapped children in America's schools.

Legal issues and problems facing school principals in the area of special needs students were viewed as a serious problem by nearly two-thirds of the respondents to the legal survey reported in chapter 2. Another 30.4 percent of the principals found that such problems were "difficult" for them as well.

Adams (2015) underscored the increasing attention being given to the rights of students with disabilities. As Adams noted, "A recent surge in complaints to the U.S. Department of Education's office for civil rights involving students with disabilities and other alleged discrimination likely stems from ramped-up outreach efforts and broader awareness of the agency's willingness to address such complaints, according to advocacy organizations, school administrators, and department officials" (p. 1). In addition, Adams's report noted that nearly half of all complaints to the civil rights office continue to involve students with disabilities, with sex- and race-discrimination complaints making up a lesser part of the caseload. This fact is supported by an examination of recent court cases in the field of education. We have discussed several court cases relative to disabled children and youth in other chapters in the book. In addition, we have included a summary of selected educational court cases during the years 2000 to 2015 in a separate section of the book.

The Education for All Handicapped Children Act of 1975 (EHA) set the stage for making certain that all students with special needs were not discriminated against in school settings. The law made it clear that students with handicaps were to be able to participate in public school programs in the same manner that other students were able to enjoy participation in educational programs and activities. Eleven years later, amendments were added to the EHA that focused on early education programs for preschool children and infants. The EDA later was named the Individuals with Disabilities Education Act (IDEA) and included the least restrictive provision whereby each disabled student was to be placed educationally so that progress in learning was assured to take place. The concept centered on the principle that every special needs student should be educated along with other students as if he or she had no disability.

The Individuals with Disabilities Education Act (IDEA) of 1990 was far reaching in that it set forth provisions to ensure that all students with disabilities could receive educational services that centered on each student's special needs. Student placement once again loomed important in the Act's provisions. School leaders were required to work with each student and parents to develop an effective Individual Education Plan that considered best placement and positive student learning progress. Individual student goals had to be determined in the best interests and needs of each individual student. The stay put provision of the law has been debated in several court cases. Best placement often was interpreted by parents to mean the highest grade or program level that the student could be placed. In one case, however, the court ruled that if the present IED program of the student revealed that the student was indeed making achievement progress, then the present statement was a satisfactory placement.

THE SCHOOL'S PARENT/STUDENT HANDBOOK AND ITS LEGAL IMPLICATIONS

A parent/student handbook is a valuable communication tool that serves as a ready reference for school procedures and well as a document for setting forth parent and student responsibilities and opportunities. Although not commonly viewed as a legal document, parent/student handbooks do include such topics as standards of dress, student discipline, damage to property, student expectations, use of iPads, and other rules that extend from such legal documents as state statutes and school board policies.

In student hearings and court cases, the court commonly asks if and how the student and parents were informed of the rule(s) in question. Evidence that the student received special instruction on the contents of the handbook and had various opportunities to ask questions about the information and rules set forth in the handbook looms important in the hearing. It has become quite common for schools to require parents to sign a form indicating that they have received and examined the handbook brought home by their child. Of course, the contents of student/parent handbooks do differ; some simply list the various school contacts that students and parents can contact for information on special topics of interest. Others are quite comprehensive and include topics from a statement of purpose of the school to dates of parent/ teacher conferences and lost and found information.

This parent/teacher handbook illustrates the leading topics for the table of contents for one school, with subtopics for the two leading topics of standard of dress and academic provisions.

Common Leading Topics for Student/Parent Handbooks

Parent/Teacher Handbook
Viewpoint East High School
Table of Contents

- Major Topics
- Academic Provisions and Requirements

  - Curriculum—Program Offerings
  - Extracurricular Programs
  - Homework Requirements
  - Grading Scale
  - Reporting Student Progress
  - Honor Roll Standards
  - Scholarship Awards/Programs
  - Testing Program

    - Subject Testing
    - State Testing Requirements
    - Intervention Program Procedures

- High School Graduation Requirements

- New Students—How to Enroll
- Absences and Tardy Guidelines
- Student Discipline
- Health Services–Nursing
- Immunizations
- Emergency Practices/Communication
- School-Sponsored Field Trips and Programs
- Parental Visitations
- Parental Conferences
- School Athletic Programs

  - Eligibility
  - Drug Testing
  - Liabilities

- Student Dress Requirements

  - Restrictions
  - Dress Expectations
  - Legal Standards
  - Physical Education Dress Requirements

- Gender Identify and Transgender Students
- Use of Electronic Equipment—Media, Student Uses
- Student Services
- Parental Involvement in School Programs
- Communication with School Personnel

  - Students
  - Parents
  - Contacting a Student's Teacher(s)
  - School Hours

- Special Needs Programs for Disabled Students

Other topics of special importance to a particular school district could be added to the handbook. We would suggest the topic of field trips be added for several important legal reasons. For instance, it looms important legally whether the students going on a field trip are considered *licensees* or *invitees*. A licensee is viewed as one that enters upon the premises by implied permission of the owner but has not been invited by the owner. On the other hand, an invitee is one who enters the premises in answer to an expressed invitation of the owner. Thus the licensee is on the property by permission, and a licensee is on the property by the invitation of the owner. In the case of the invitee, the owner must take special means to take special care for the safety of the individual while on the premises. In cases of court rulings, licensees that are injured on an owner's property had no rights for injury damages. Invitees are given the assurance of an observed degree of care, precaution, and vigilance in relation to the degree that circumstances demand such protection.

In many parent/student handbooks, the school's mission statement and its primary purposes are included in the handbook. School leaders that take special means to inform and update students and parents on school rules will realize positive results in the way of fewer violations and the positive outcomes.

Snapshot #1 Who Is Liable for Student Injuries?

Tort liability is generally defined as a civil wrong whereby one person injures another person physically or perhaps libels or slanders one's reputation. When one fails to conform to certain standards required to protect other persons, fails to act according to expected standards, causes injury due to the fact that he or she did not act according to expected standards, or there is a specific loss to an individual as the result of an injury caused by another, then liability is likely to constitute a tort.

Consider the following scenarios. Which entries are likely tort liability cases?

1. A school grade school teacher is coaxed into playing softball with his sixth-grade class during recess. He hits a ball that strikes a boy student in the eye. The boy's injury requires the treatment by an ophthalmologist.

2. During the noon hour at a senior high school, students were left to use the playground or school gym for various activities. Commonly, there was at least one teacher that was "on duty" to give general supervision during this time. A recreational game of basketball often took place in the gym and allowed each player to wear a boxing glove on one hand during the game.

   If a player was dribbling down the court, it was common for an opponent to hit the player with the boxing glove and try to steal the basketball at the same time. On one occasion, a player hit another and that player tripped and fell to the floor, knocking him unconscious. The boy suffered cuts on his face and head and also suffered a concussion.

3. The driving education teacher was riding with one of his student drivers, who was at the wheel. Two other students were observing from the back seat of the car. The student driver was driving under the speed limit but missed seeing a roadside warning sign that read, "Keep to the left." As a result, the student drove through a roadblock sign and went into a ditch that was part of the street work in that lane. The two students in the back were not wearing their seat belts and were thrown forward in the car. One struck the teacher in the front seat, and both suffered injuries that required a doctor's attention.

4. Although the lettermen's club initiation had been ruled as forbidden in the school gymnasium and school grounds, the lettermen in the school decided to hold the initiation of new members anyway but off school grounds. Word of the off-campus initiation soon got around, and the school sports coach informed the school principal that an initiation of some kind apparently was underway off school grounds. The principal expressed the view that the school could not control the outside events of everything that students might do on their own. Seven of the eleven students that were eligible for club membership showed up for the initiation on one weekend. During the initiation, one student fell from a city water tower and suffered a broken back.

5. Two unruly ninth-grade students were seen in a classroom playing keepaway with a home economics teacher's purse. The female teacher would run back and forth between the two male students with her hands in the air in an attempt to catch the purse. Another male teacher walked by the classroom and saw what was going on. He rushed inside the classroom and yelled at the boys to halt what they were doing. The largest ninth-grader once again threw the purse over the male teacher's head. In turn, the male teacher tackled the student and pounced on him. Both hit the floor, but the student's head hit the floor. His injuries were such that the home economics teacher called 911.

The points to be considered in each of the foregoing scenarios depend on several factors. However, the following comments underscore the elements that most always serve to determine the outcomes of tort liability cases against the teacher and/or school officials. Did the teacher do something that should have or should not have been done?

1. Did the defendant in the case have a responsibility/duty to protect the plaintiff against the risk of injury?
2. Did the defendant fail to carry out his/her responsibilities regarding protection against damage and/or injury?

3. Were the results of the injury due specifically to the fact that the defendant did not carry out his or her expected/required responsibilities?

In brief, was negligence expressly shown by the defendant's failure to act as a prudent person would have acted in the same situation? As noted by Nolte (1973):

1. Did the defendant or defendants owe the plaintiff a duty?
2. Was there a breach of the duty owed?
3. Was the breach the proximate cause of the injury? (p. 139)

A WORD ABOUT NEGLIGENCE

Negligence is failure to exercise the proper degree of care in a specific situation. Thus, a teacher is expected to exercise the care that an individual of ordinary wisdom and prudence would demonstrate in similar circumstances. It appears imperative that school leaders and faculty personnel give thought to the possibilities of "danger" relative to an undertaking being considered. For example, the teacher's science class is planning a field trip to a recently discovered cave now open to the public. A schoolteacher is assigned to chaperone a student party where social dancing will be permitted. The teacher is accompanying three students to a university-sponsored journalism workshop. A school car will be provided for transportation.

A fifth-grade boy is hit by a baseball pitched by another student during a fifth- and sixth-grade competitive baseball game. The teacher is serving as umpire for the game. A chemistry student is working in the science lab. Her hair gets too close to the Bunsen burner and the girl's hair catches fire. The girl suffers facial and head burns. What precautions should the teachers in each of these cases have taken before and during the actual implementation of each of these activities, if any? Suppose the students in the fifth-and-sixth-grade baseball game did not have baseball helmets to wear while batting. What liabilities might be alleged?

In any case, in the foregoing situations, the teacher has the legal responsibility of informing the student(s) before possible injury does occur. In any situation in which the student faces possible danger or injury, the teacher must inform the student and take whatever steps necessary to protect the safety of the student. When the lack of supervision is the likely cause of injury, the teacher is personally liable under those cases for any injuries suffered by students. Most authorities recommend that teachers carry personal insurance to protect his or her liability in the event of student accidents since students do have accidents and teachers are always with students.

LEGAL CASES COMMONLY CONJURE UP THE WORD *ETHICS*: WHAT, IF ANY, LEGAL IMPLICATIONS ARE IMPORTANT?

Webster defines the term *ethics* as involving or expressing moral approval or disapproval; conforming to professional standards of conduct; or the principles of conduct governing an individual or group. The term centers on what is professionally right or correct in relation to professional standards of conduct. The National Education Association adopted a code of ethics more than eighty years ago and since has revised the code on several occasions.

The American Association of School Personnel Administrators approved a statement of ethics for personnel administrators in 2003. Of the ten statements of standards listed in the code, five of them centered on specific legal behaviors: (1) supports the principle of due process and protects the civil and human rights of all individuals, (2) obeys local, state, and national laws and does not join or support organizations that advocate, directly or indirectly, the overthrow of the government, (3) implements the Board of Education's policies and administrative regulations, (4) pursues appropriate measures to correct those laws, policies, and regulations that are not consistent with accepted educational goals, and (5) honors all contracts until fulfilled or released.

TIME OUT! PRE-QUIZ ON STUDENT RIGHTS

Take a few minutes to take the following pre-quiz on students' rights relative to such matters as student dress, placement, suspension, and other matters.

1. A mentally handicapped student came to school late one morning. The teacher observed that he was unstable and acting rather strangely. He was taken to the school nurse who observed the boy and came to the conclusion that he obviously was under the influence of alcohol or some illegal drug. The school principal sent him home under the supervision of the school's security officer, who informed his guardians that the student was being recommended to the school board for expulsion. The school has the authority to expel this student regardless of the fact that the student's behavior was found to be related to his handicap. ____T or ____F

2. It is clear now that a student's dress for school is controlled by the student's parents. School officials have no authority to regulate student dress. ____T or ____F

3. To protect himself against any liability, a teacher asks that every student obtain a permission slip for him or her to attend a science field trip. Thus, when signed by the parent, the student has no claim for

injuries that might occur on such a school-sponsored trip. ____T or ____F

4. A school established the practice of opening each school day with a recorded prayer over the school's speaker system. Students were not required to say the prayer but were required to stand in silence while others bowed their heads and said the prayer. Since the student was not required to say the prayer, the courts would support this practice. ____T or ____F

5. A public school student was attending a school that was failing in providing a quality educational program for its students. The student then reenrolled in another private school under a voucher program established by the state. The voucher program will pay for the student's tuition fees for attending the other school. ____T or ____F

6. A parent challenged the Individual Education Program (IEP) set forth for her child. The court will expect the school officials to prove that the present program is appropriate for the student. ____T or ____F

7. A senior high school female becomes pregnant and is not married. A school principal recommends that she be placed in a homeschooling program and not be allowed to participate in any school extracurricular activities. The court will support this decision if the student and/or parents file a lawsuit regarding this decision. ____T or ____F

8. A public school student was suspended from school for ten school days due to a behavior violation of the school's rules. In such cases, the school is authorized to suspend the student without further administrative action. ____T or ____F

9. A student wants to participate in the school's football program, but he and his parents refuse to take part in the drug-testing program required by school board policy. If a lawsuit is filed, the court will most likely support the parents since the medication requirements for any child should be within the authority of the child when under the age of eighteen. ____T or ____F

10. A student that was denied the right of procedural due process is entitled to nominal damages even if his or her suspension is found to be justified. ____T or ____F

11. Although parents can be involved in special education court cases, they are required by law to have a qualified lawyer handle the case. ____T or ____F

12. Serious student violations such as the use of illegal drugs on campus commonly lead to suspension. In such cases, courts continue to rule in favor of the school officials by stating that due process procedures are "without reason" since the evidence is clear on the surface. ____T or ____F

13. School principals have been authorized to "just use best judgment" when receiving calls or reports of matters such as bomb threats or school invasion since the large majority (92 percent) of such calls have proven to be pranks and unfounded. ____T or ____F

14. Bullying in schools has been considered as "normal behavior" by the courts, and thus the courts have "refused" to consider further cases. ____T or ____F

15. The courts have ruled compulsory pupil attendance as constitutional since it is the responsibility of parents to educate their children. ____T or ____F

Answer to the Quiz: #1, #2, #3, #4, #6, #7, #8, #9, #11, #12, #13, #14, and #15 are False. #5 and #10 are True.

Discussion of the Pre-Quiz

#1 In considering expulsion for a handicapped student, special consideration must be given to the nature of his or her handicap. Thus, question #1 is false. In the court case of *Honig v. Doe* (484 U.S. 305, 1988), the court ruled strongly for protecting students with handicaps. Specifically, the court stated that "schools shall not expel children for behaviors related to their handicaps." Thus, school principals must exercise caution when suspending or expelling students with special needs because the courts place the burden of proof on the school in determining if the behavior was the result of the student's disability.

#2 In regard to student dress and hair styling, school officials are authorized to control such matters on the part of the student if they are disruptive, immodest, or vulgar. If the hairstyle becomes a safety issue or is a disturbance for other students, the school principal has the authority to ask for changes. Certain sayings on T-shirts have been ruled inappropriate or unconstitutional by the courts as well. The court cases *Broussard v. School Board of Norfolk* (1992) and *Morse v. Frederick* (2007), previously discussed, centered on the wearing of T-shirts with inappropriate illegal drug use and religious implications.

In the case of *Scott v. Board of Education, Union Free School District #17* (1969), the court ruled that the school authorities did have certain control over the dress of students. School rules that were intended to protect human safety or control disruption were acceptable. The wearing of slacks, although not prohibited, could be prohibited by the school board if they brought "undue attention" to anatomical details or were especially "distasteful."

#3 A permission slip from parents for a student to participate in an off-campus activity does not release a teacher from the possibility of negligence. Although asking parents to sign a permission slip does have merit, reasonable care and safety provisions on the part of the teacher are expected. Informing students of the potential dangers associated with a field trip and instructing the participants about the precautions that should be kept in mind would be positive actions in case an unforeseen student accident did occur.

Liability centers on the question of negligence on the part of the schoolteacher in charge. If a student is injured due to an unforeseen accident that could not have been avoided, the teacher generally would not be held responsible for the injury. Failure to provide the necessary instruction for an activity before having students participate also leaves the teacher in an indefensible position if a student injury does occur. In some cases, students should be given the option of participating or not participating in new and challenging activities due to the possibility of injury.

#4 There have been numerous court cases on prayer in schools. "Forcing" a student to participate in any way in prayer or religious activities in public schools is unconstitutional. Requiring a student to stand in silence during a prayer is a violation of their First Amendment rights. However, an 1884 court case ruled that students were permitted to meet on school grounds to discuss religion after school (*Westside Community Schools v. Mergens* [1990]). The court did not view this activity as a state-sponsored religious activity. Since the school had previously approved other after-school interest clubs and activities, it could prohibit religious clubs.

#5 In those instances in which a student is attending a school rated as failing, underperforming, or another unsatisfactory student achievement level, courts have ruled that the parents can receive another school and be eligible for the state's voucher program. There have been several other court cases in which a plaintiff has claimed that the school did not give him or her a free and appropriate education. In one case, *Donohue v. Copiague Union Free School District* (1979), the appellant claimed that he lacked the ability to comprehend written English even though he had received passing and/or minimal grades during his educational experiences. The court ruled in favor of the school district, stating that to attempt to judge "educational malpractice" would not only require the court to make judgments about past practices but also that to keep a day-to-day record of such causes of action would lead to "blatant interference" with the responsibilities of local administrators. Courts have consistently avoided their involvement in matters of administration best left to the local school administrators and Boards of Education.

#6 In those cases in which parents complain or challenge provisions of their child's Individual Educational Plan (IEP), the courts have expected the parents, not the school officials, to prove that the present program is not appropriate for the child (*Schaffer v. Weast*, 546 U.S. [2005]). If property done, the parents, teachers, child, and school principal have been involved in the completion of the child's educational plan. If the parent has been omitted from the process, the courts commonly will indicate that this failure is a violation of the Children with Disabilities Act. In addition, if the child is making academic progress with the educational plan in place, it most likely will approve the continuation of the present plan. Parents do not have the authority to decide the placement of their child. However, if the child is not making some progress in the present educational placement, the court will likely rule on the need for a review.

#7 A pregnant student is permitted to continue her educational program and participate in all extracurricular activities if such involvement is supported by the student's physician. In the case of *Davis v. Meeks* (1972), the court ruled that marital, maternal, or paternal status shall not affect the rights and privileges of students to receive a public education nor to take part in any extracurricular activity offered by the school. In addition, students may participate in school programs and activities regardless of their past or present marital status. *Holt v. Shelton* (1972) approved the continuation of pregnant students in all instances when the pregnant student had the approval of her physician.

#8 Student suspension procedures differ among the fifty states. However, it appears that any suspension of more than three days requires some form of due process. It is clear that a student's suspension must be carried out according to state statutes. In regard to question #8, it would seem wise for the school to administer the suspension case through a due process procedure. One state ruled that a suspension that exceeded five days would require a due process procedure. Another case noted that when even a short period of time was given in suspension that a statement of charges and a due process hearing were in order. Of course, the wise thing to do as school principal is to know the exact provisions of student suspension set forth by state statutes and by the local Board of Education and follow them to the letter.

#9 The requirement of drug testing for participation in public school sports programs has been clearly decided by court rulings. A student that refuses to participate in the school district's required drug testing can prohibit the student's participation in sports without worry about a rights violation. In the *Vernonia School District v. Acton* (1995) court case, the parents of a student argued that requiring a drug test when there was no evidence of illegal drug abuse was a violation of the Fourth Amendment of search and seizure. The court ruled otherwise, indicating that schools must keep school campuses safe and free from drugs. The importance of caring for the safe environment of the school and keeping athletes away from drugs outweighed the small invasion of privacy necessitated by a drug test. Similar rulings have been set forth regarding the requirements of immunizations. The courts have been consistent in protecting the safety and welfare of pupils in public schools.

#10 The answer to question #10 is based on the court's ruling in the case of *Carey v. Piphus* (435 U.S. 247, 1978). The case involved students that were denied due process procedures when suspended from school. In this rather "detailed and complicated case," the court's final ruling indicted that students should receive only "nominal damages" and not "substantial punitive damages" when suspended without due process proceedings, even when the reason for suspension is withheld. Suspension in any case results in considerable stress and mental disturbance on the part of the accused.

#11 The Supreme Court of the United States has ruled that parents do not have to hire a qualified lawyer in special education cases. That is, parents can serve for the defense of their child. In the case of *Winkelman v. Parma City School District* (No. 05-983, 2007), the Supreme Court ruled that parents may represent their own children in special education cases and do not need to hire a lawyer for court purposes.

#12 Due process of the law as set forth in the Fourteenth Amendment of the U.S. Constitution is important in all cases of student suspension. Regardless of the conditions surrounding student violations such as the illegal use of drugs, due process looms important. The right of due process is to provide a fair chance for the defendant to present his or her side of the story. The use of the term *without reason* in question number 12 is meaningless.

#13 School principals certainly should not follow the "false advice" set forth in question #13. There are recommendations for handling such occurrences as bomb threats. Even though most bomb calls are "false threats," it is necessary to take steps in the name of student and personnel safety. Most school districts have emergency booklets that set forth the specific procedures that should be followed in cases such as bomb threat, school intruders with a weapon, serious weather storms, serious student injury, and other emergencies. The emergency booklets are marked with reference labels for easy access to various situations and the step-by-step procedures that are to be followed in each instance.

We take time here to describe bomb threat procedures set forth in an article on the web (July 25, 2015). The following procedures are for information purposes only and not set forth as the right thing to do for every school situation. That is, the procedures are suggestive in nature and might be helpful to others in developing bomb procedures for their respective schools. The procedures are summarized as follows.

In the event school personnel receive a call indicating that there is a bomb in the school, the following procedures should be followed:

1. The individual receiving the call should remain calm, be courteous, and listen carefully for details. If the caller remains on the line after the initial statement is made, ask questions such as "Where is the bomb?" "What does it look like?" and the name of the person calling should be asked. The exact time of the call should be noted.

2. Follow the appropriate call trace or caller identification procedures. Such procedures are to be kept by each telephone that is a direct access line.
3. The person receiving the call should immediately notify the building principal or designee in his/her absence. The person receiving the call is to talk to no one other than as instructed by the building principal or designee.
4. The building principal or the person designated should notify the police of the bomb threat by calling the police phone number and the local fire department.
5. The school office secretary should notify the superintendent of schools of the bomb threat. The office of the superintendent will notify other schools that the school has received a bomb threat just to alert them of such a potential call.
6. The school principal or designee must decide if the school is to be evacuated. If the caller provided a specific time when the device was to explode, the building should be evacuated immediately.
7. Teachers are always to carry their student roll books with them to assure student accountability.
8. The school principal is to request that the police and fire department personnel inspect the building for the bomb.
9. The principal and police/fire personnel will determine when it is safe for students and staff to return to the building.
10. A bomb threat report form should be completed by the person who received the call and the administrative action that was taken for the safety of the students and staff personnel.

In addition, the emergency booklet should include the steps for tracing a call as provided by the police department or other local governmental office. In most cases, the procedure is brief: Immediately following the call, press the release receiver button. At the dial tone, press the number given to the school for tracing calls. Listen for confirmation and then hang up. Notify the principal, police, and superintendent's office, who will notify others that must be informed.

#14 The problem of bullying, on the contrary, has been viewed as most serious by courts nationally. The liability of negligence on the part of school principals and teachers has been considered in a number of court cases. However, court cases on bullying are "complicated" and in some cases close with indefinite rulings. One example is that of *T. K. v. New York Department of Education* (E.D. New York, April 2011). The case is far too involved and complicated to be detailed here. In brief, the complaint was that a student, T. K., was deprived of an appropriate education because her school reportedly did nothing to prevent her from being so bullied by other students that her education opportunities were reduced. The plaintiff argued that the Individuals with Disabilities Education Act gave assurances for an appropriate education for disabled students. Bullying makes the education environment "hostile." The several court dispositions on this matter reportedly consisted of eighty-two pages.

The outcome of the court's opinions appears to rest on several factors: (1) the plaintiff has proved that he or she was harassed due to his or her disability, (2) the harassment (bullying) was such that it was a factor in inhibiting the opportunity for an education, (3) the defendant was aware of the harassment, and (4) the school officials knew of the harassment and was indifferent to the harassment. Two other cases on bulling are worthy of note. In the case of *Kowalski v. Berkeley County Schools* (No. 10-1098, 4th Cir., 2011), a student was ridiculed by another student on the Internet. The student that posted the criticism on the web was suspended. The student sued on the basis that it violated her freedom of speech. Both the U.S. District Court and the U.S. Court of Appeals upheld the school's authority to discipline speech that interfered with the requirements of the school to control the discipline needed to operate the school's program.

In the case of *Hannibal Public Schools v. D.J.M.* (U.S. District Court, Missouri, 2:08CV63 JCH), a student sent messages to fellow classmates that suggested that he could obtain a gun and speculated whom he might shoot. The situation reached the school principal's office and the school superintendent was informed; the superintendent called police. D. J. M. was placed under juvenile detention and transferred to a hospital for psychiatric examination.

#15 Historically, the child's parents have controlled school attendance. In early 1796, courts noted that if they chose for their child not to attend school, the court could not force them to do so. This all changed by the early 1900s, when the courts gave states the authority to control such educational matters.

Attendance depends largely on state statutes and various rulings by the courts. The matter of attendance is left primarily to the local school board as long as the board does not violate the provisions of state statutes. Approximately ninety years ago, attendance by children and youth in schools was viewed as compulsory by a court in Tennessee (*Scopes v. State of Tennessee* 289 S.W. 363, 1927). The court stated that if pupils did not volunteer to attend school that they could be compelled to do so. Another court stated specifically that parents were "duty bound" to see that their child was in school. In fact, schooling was imposed on the pupil for the good of the public. Schooling served to protect the state from the results of an ignorant and incompetent citizenry (Nolte, 1973).

In any case, student attendance is a serious legal problem for school principals; approximately 75 percent of school principals viewed attendance as a "serious problem" or a "difficult problem" in the legal survey reported in chapter 2.

The U.S. Department of Education has answered several key questions regarding the rights of parents for access to their child's education records. Specific rights and restrictions are set forth in the Family Educational Rights and Privacy Act (FERPA) of 1974.

YOU BE THE JUDGE: BRIEF SCENARIOS TO THINK ABOUT

Several brief scenarios are set forth in the following section. You are to serve as the judge in giving a ruling in each case. Note that the scenarios are based on actually known cases that have been decided by school boards and in courts of law. After reading the information/facts related to each case, give your ruling in support of the plaintiff or defendant. In addition, take time to justify your decision. The actual court ruling in each case is given later in the chapter. You might find the information gained in this chapter and in the previous chapters of the book to be helpful to you in making a decision. If so, it is OK to use these "similar case" rulings to make your judgments.

Please understand that each of the following cases are far more involved than is possible to describe here. Only a few key facts of each case are set forth. For our purposes, however, the brief scenarios serve our intentions; the exercise should help each reader think about occurrences that do take place realistically in education and the fact that judgments are based on the protections of the rights of accused and the reasonableness of the actions of persons in positions of responsibility.

Case Scenario #1 Student Dress

In this case, the legal question focused on the wearing of slacks by female students. The Board of Education objected to the wearing of slacks because of the undue attention and disruption that they caused. The Board members were of the opinion that they had the right to prohibit the wearing of slacks.

Your Ruling as Judge: Judgment for the Plaintiff (Student)_____; Judgment for the Defendant (Board)_____.

Rationale for your Opinion:

Case Scenario #2 Discipline Treatment of a Five-Year-Old Student

A behaviorally disorderly five-year-old child allegedly was tied to his desk by the tenured school principal. The pupil's ankles and wrists were bound with duct tape, and he reportedly was left in an open doorway in public view for an estimated two hours. The school board demoted the principal to classroom teacher, and the teacher filed a lawsuit against the school superintendent for her demotion. A hearing was held and a board member participated in the tenure hearing. The school board did not make taped witness statements available to the principal before the hearing. The pupil's medical records were not made available to the principal before the hearing, and the defendant voiced other due process concerns. In the lawsuit filed by the teacher, the defendant stated that the demotion was biased and capricious and violated her rights of due process under the Fourteenth Amendment.

Your Ruling as Judge: Judgment for the Plaintiff____; Judgment for the Defendant _____.

Rationale for Your Opinion:

Case Scenario #3 Student Locker Searches

A high school student's locker was searched by police officers after the principal and the student did not object to the search. The officers brought the contents of the locker to the principal's office, and they found a key among the contents. The student claimed that the key was for a locker in another city, and he hadn't had the opportunity to retrieve the contents. The officers called the site where the locker was supposed to be and learned that there was no such locker. It was learned that the key was for another locker elsewhere. In searching that locker, illegal drugs and money were found. All of this investigation was tied to a robbery that had taken place in the city.

The student and his attorney argued that the student's rights of "search and seizure" had been violated; the student had control of his locker and the original search was a violation of his rights.

Your Ruling as Judge: Judgment for the Plaintiff____; Judgment for the Defendant_____.

Rationale for Your Opinion:

Case Scenario #4 Corporal Punishment in Public Schools

A student was given corporal punishment for the violation of a stated classroom rule. The student and parents filed a lawsuit against the school principal. The mother previously told the principal that her son was a frail child and that she herself did not believe in corporal punishment. She argued that her son's rights under the Fourteenth Amendment had been violated under the due process clause.

Your Ruling as Judge: Judgment for the Plaintiff____; Judgment for the Defendant____.

Rationale for Your Opinion:

Case Scenario #5 Married Students and School Participation

Davis was a high school student and a quality baseball player. He was scholastically an honors student. He was eighteen years of age and got a sixteen-year-old girl pregnant. She later had a miscarriage. The student married the girl. The school Board of Education ruled that married students could not participate in extracurricular activities. Davis filed a lawsuit against excluding him from participating in school activities and sought damages. The school board passed a rule that married students could not participate in extracurricular activities apparently after the fact. Meeks, president of the school board, argued that married pupils are not permitted to participate in school-sponsored extracurricular activities, including the junior-senior prom.

Davis contended that he had the right to get married and that the board's action violated his civil rights.

Your Ruling as Judge: Judgment for the Plaintiff____; Judgment for the Defendant____.

Rationale for Your Opinion:

Case Scenario #6 Student Vaccinations

A city ordinance stated that no child or other person could attend a public or private school without being able to present a certificate of vaccination. A girl that did not have a certificate of vaccinations and refused to be vaccinated was not allowed to attend school. The student argued that there was really no medical reason at the time to have to be vaccinated and the law was overly controlling in its requirements. A lawsuit was filed and heard by a court of law.

Your Ruling as Judge: Judgment for the student (Plaintiff)____; Judgment for the Defendant____.

Rationale for Your Opinion:

Rulings on Scenario Cases #1 to #6

Scenario #1—Student Dress. The court ruled in favor of the school district. In the case of *Scott v. Board of Education, Union Free School District #17* (1969), the court stated that school dress that causes undue attention and disruption may be regulated by the school officials. However, a "flat prohibition" of the wearing of slacks is not valid.

Scenario #2—Discipline of Student and the Principal's Demotion. This scenario centered on the court case of *Sylvester v. Cancienne* (95-0789, P.7 La.App. 1st Cir., November 9, 1995, 664 So. 2d 1259, 1263). The court upheld the demotion of the principal and ruled that the school board did not arbitrarily and capriciously act in finding the principal guilty of incompetency and willful neglect. In addition, the court ruled that the school board had not denied the principal procedural due process.

Scenario #3—Student Locker Search. Several court cases have ruled using a similar rationale. School officials are authorized to search a student's locker when there is reasonable evidence that the search is warranted. In the case of *State v. Stein* (203 Kan, 638, 456 P. 2nd; Cert denied, 90S. Ct. 996, 1970), courts have ruled that the student does not have control of the locker inclusively against school officials. Reasonable searches are authorized when there is sufficient evidence to suspect that a search will result in finding what is expected to be inside the locker.

Scenario #4—Corporal Punishment. The use of corporal punishment in all cases depends on two key factors. First, is corporal punishment permitted by state statues and school board policies? If not, corporal punishment cannot be administered in any instance. If corporal punishment is permitted, the question of reasonableness looms important. Have all other discipline options been exhausted? Does the severity of the case and the history of the student's behavior lend support to the use of corporal punishment? In view of the "lack of evidence" set forth in Scenario #4, the use of corporal punishment is questionable.

Scenario #5—Married Student and School Participation. The student in this case should be awarded every opportunity to participate in a quality education program and to participate in school sports programs unless some state statute or athletic association regulations prohibit his participation. In the case of *Davis V. Meeks* (344 F. Supp. 298 [N.P. Oho, 1972]), it was ruled that marital, maternal, or paternal status shall not affect the right and privilege of students to take part in any extracurricular activities offered by the school or to participate in a regular school program.

Scenario #6—Student Vaccinations. Courts have been consistent in authorizing school districts to require vaccinations in relation to human diseases and also drug testing of students, especially for those students that wish to participate in the school's athletic programs. Refusal to get required vaccinations is a reason for prohibiting a student to attend school. The courts have historically viewed the welfare and safety of all students to be among the first priorities of school program objectives.

KEY IDEAS AND RECOMMENDATIONS SET FORTH IN CHAPTER 4

- Student personnel matters loom significant relative to the legal responsibilities of school leaders and other professionals. Educators must have a good knowledge of legal rulings for decision making and the responsible operations of the school. Knowing and understanding the wide variety of "issues" that have been judged by the various state and federal courts serve a positive purpose for the school principal and his or her decision-making responsibilities.

- Legal cases/rulings cover a wide range of student behaviors and rights in the educational setting. Being knowledgeable in this area of school responsibilities will result in a reduced level of legal problems that most likely would be encountered otherwise.

- The foundational rulings of the nation's courts reflect the constitutional rights of students, and these rulings have implications for the rights and liabilities of students in America's schools.

- School boards and school personnel do have the authority to control the environment of public schools in the best interests of education and the welfare of students.

- Laws do differ among the states, and laws are changed periodically by decisions of superior courts. In addition, court rulings are not always unanimous. One example is that of corporal punishment, whereby the U.S. Supreme Court ruled that corporal punishment was constitutional by a vote of 5 to 4.

- Historically, the courts have tended to allow local school boards to control the operations/decisions regarding public school matters. Nevertheless, the federal government has mandated numerous regulations for local school procedures as a condition for receiving federal funds.

- It is obvious that religion practices are forbidden in public school programs. Praying in school, religious "talks" on school premises if sponsored by the school, religious plaques/newspapers, and other activities are viewed as unconstitutional. On the other hand, if a school has approved various after-school clubs and programs, courts have approved a student religious club in the school.

- Corporal punishment in the school is OK according to the U.S. Supreme Court. The Court has placed this matter in the hands of each state. However, corporal punishment must be reasonable, and law forbids abusive punishment.

- Without question, student suspension and expulsion require the implementation of due process procedures. Three underlying principles of effective school law are fairness, reasonableness, and competence. Reasonableness is not quite as simple to implement as it might seem. If the action taken was indeed "reasonable," is always determined after the fact. What might appear to be reasonable by one person might be viewed as abusive by another party. From a "legal" point of view, a reasonable action appears to be viewed by the answer to the question: "Was the behavior taken such that it would be the behavior/action taken by any other person under the circumstances?"

- The value of information and effective communication regarding student/ parent expectations is of paramount importance. A comprehensive parent/ student handbook has proven of great benefit for giving directions for student and parent behaviors relative to educational purposes.
- The term *negligence* looms important in the behaviors of school leaders and professional staff personnel. When professional negligence on the part of a principal or teacher is shown in evidence, the court's ruling is most certain to be against them.
- Informing the teacher, students, classified personnel, and parents of the school district's policies, school district regulations and the state's educational statutes are a responsibility of the school principal.

DISCUSSION QUESTIONS

1. First, consider your opinion on case 4.1 and the status of the action that appears to be the consensus of the school faculty. What might you have added to the discussion if you were in a position to do so?
2. What, if anything, do the comments and behaviors of the school members tell us about their knowledge of school law in relation to corporal punishment and court rulings?
3. Assume that Principal Alexander does talk to the district school superintendent about this case. Also, assume that the school superintendent is quite knowledgeable about school law and teaches a class on the subject for the local community college. What do you surmise that the superintendent will say to Principal Alexander?
4. What court cases or court rulings do you consider to be the most significant for student personnel, and why?
5. Group Activity: Divide the group into teams of four persons, and have each team take a pro or con stance to debate the proposition: Cyberbullying for the most part is no more than teasing or "games that students play. That's just what kids do."

CASE STUDIES

Case Study #4.1

Harry is a sixth-grade student at Wymore Elementary School. When in grade 5, he was suspended for three days for bullying. Although his bullying lessened during the remainder of that school year, it was witnessed once again at the beginning of grade 6. His sixth-grade teacher, Mrs. Deardoff, indicated that the boy was intolerable and nothing that she could do to control his unruly behavior had been effective so far.

A security guard had reported that a fifth-grade student told him that Harry had taken his lunch money on two occasions. He was told that if he reported this to his parents or to the school that he would "be in for it." When school recess teams were chosen for baseball or volleyball, Harry was commonly chosen first. He was the biggest kid in grade 6, and reportedly he got upset when a team captain did not choose him first.

The state's statutes forbid corporal punishment. The school board had not acted policywise regarding the matter of corporal punishment.

At the after-school faculty meeting, Harry's sixth-grade teacher brought up the matter of Harry and his obtrusive behavior. Most everyone at the meeting had some thoughts about Harry.

Assistant Principal Delmar Gould, commented, "Suspension didn't work last year and I would guess that it would be an exercise in futility if we tried that remedy again this year. What I think he needs is a few whacks on his behind. I have reason enough to do that job myself!"

Principal Rodriquez noted that state statutes forbid corporal punishment.

"Yes, but the nation's Supreme Court doesn't prohibit corporal punishment," said Mrs. Deardoff, Harry's teacher. "Doesn't that Court have the final say on the matter of corporal punishment?"

"Well," said Principal Alexander. "I agree with the recommendation that has been stated, but let me check with the district office before we move ahead on this matter. I will report back ASAP."

REFERENCES

Adams, C. J. (2015, May 20). Special education students swell civil rights docket. *Education Week.* http://www.edweek.org/ew/articles/2015/05/20/special-education-students-swell-civil-rights-docket.html.

Bednar, W. D., Jr. (1984). *School law update: Preventive school law.* NOLPE, 37, 22–29.

Dunklee, D. R. (1985). An assessment of knowledge about tort liability law as possessed by selected public school teachers and principals. Doctoral dissertation, Kansas University, 1982. *Dissertation Abstracts International* 78, 2801.

Jacobs, T. (2008, September 15). *10 Supreme Court cases every teen should know. New York Times,* September 2007.

Lynch, H. Lewis, & Kuehl, Ray. (1983). Recent graduates have definite ideas on how to improve teacher education programs. *Teacher Evaluator* 59, 168–72.

Mississippi Department of Education. (2006, June). *School law primer for educators and school personnel: Everything you need to know about school law and how it affects the school environment.* Office of Healthy Schools, Jackson, MS: Author.

Nolte, M. C. (1973). *Duties and liabilities of school administrators.* West Nyack, NY: Parker Publishing Company, Inc.

Norton, M. S. (2015). *The principal as human resources leader: A guide to exemplary practices for personnel administration.* New York: Routledge.

Norton, M. S., Kelly, L. K., & Battle, A. R. (2012). *The principal as student advocate: Doing what's best for all students.* Larchmont, NY: Eye on Education.

Ogletree, R., & Gauett, K. C. (1981). *Essentials of school law.* New York: Appleton.

Peterson, L. J., Rossmiller, R. A., & Volz, M. M. (1978). *The law and public school operation.* New York: Harper & Row Publishers Inc.

Sametz, L., McLoughlin, C., & Streib, V. (1983). Legal education for preservice teachers: Basic or remediation? *Journal of Teacher Education* 34, 10–12.

Sorenson, G. P., & Chapman, D. W. (1985). School compliance with federal law concerning the release of student records. *Educational Evaluation and Policy Analysis* 7, 9–18.

Staver, M. D. (2005). Teachers' rights on public school campuses. Chapter 4 in *Eternal vigilance knowing and protecting your religious freedom.* Nashville, TN: Broadman & Holman Publishers.

Stein, N. (2013). Q & A with Nan Stein, Ed.D.: Educators can make a difference in preventing gender-based violence. *Research & Action* (Spring/Summer 2013). Wellesley: MA: Wellesley Centers for Women.

Thanawala, S. (2015, June 5). Student wears eagle feather at graduation after lawsuit. *The Fresno Bee.*

United States Department of Health & Human Services. (2015, August 5). *What is cyberbullying?*

Webwise. (2015, August 5). *Dealing with cyberbullying in schools.* http://www.webwise.ie/teachers/dealing-with-cyberbullying-in-schools-2/.

Wikipedia, (2015, June 19). *Santa Fe Independent School District v. Doe.* https://en.wikipedia.org/wiki/Santa_Fe_Independent_School_District_v._Doe.

Appendix A: Recent Educational Court Cases from the Years 2000 to 2015

I. SPECIAL EDUCATION AND STUDENTS WITH DISABILITIES

Amanda v. Clark Co. Sch. Dist. & Nevada Dept. of Ed. (9th Cir., 2001)—District's need to provide formal written offer regarding educational placement.

Anchorage School District v. MP (9th Cir., 2002)—Requirement for school district to comply with IDEA provisions.

Arlington Central School District v. Pearl and Theodore Murphy (548 U.S., 2006)—Parents that hire experts in cases concerned with the Individuals with Disabilities Education Act cannot be reimbursed for fees expended for their services.

Bd. of Educ. of City Sch. Dist. of New York v. Tom F. (2007)—Can parents receive reimbursement for fees expended when a child, who never received services in a public school, can do so when attending a private school?

Doug C. v. Hawaii (9th Circuit Court, 2013)—Parental participation in Individualized Educational Program (IEP) meeting.

Forest Grove School District v. T.A. (2009)—Does IDEA allow reimbursement for services rendered by a private school even when such services were not rendered in a former public school?

Goleta Union Elementary School Dist. v. Andrew Ordway (C.D. Cal., 2002)—Federal judge ruled that a Santa Barbara high school administrator was personally liable for damages under the Civil Rights Act for violating a mother's right to get a free and appropriate public education for her special needs son.

HH v. Moffett & Chesterfield School Bd. (4th Cir., 2009)—Abusive treatment of disabled child violated the child's rights under the Fourteenth Amendment and therefore the appellant was not entitled to immunity.

Jaynes v. Newport News Public School Bd. (4th Cir., 2001)—Autistic child receives home-based program and considerations of related statutes, procedures, notices, and reimbursements.

Joseph James v. Upper Arlington Sch. District (6th Cir., 2000)—Tuition reimbursement for child with dyslexia.

Knable v. Bexley City Sch. District (6th Cir., 2001)—Disabled child and burden of proof related to IEPs and other requirements.

PV v. Philadelphia (U.S. District Court, 2013)—Focused on violation of changing a disabled child's placement without convening IEP meetings, excluding parents', and other violations of IDEA.

Winkelman v. Parma City School District (No. 5-983, 2007)—Parents do not have to hire an attorney for court appearances. Parents are entitled to represent their child's interests.

II. STUDENT DISCIPLINE AND SUSPENSION

Community Consolidated Sch. Dist. #93 v. John F. (IL) (N.D. IL, 2000)—Consideration of several violations in a student discipline case and appropriate services to a disabled child.

III. CHILD ABUSE BY SCHOOL PERSONNEL

A.C. et al. v. Shelby County (6th Cir., 2013)—Principal filed false abuse allegations against child's parents.

Covington v. Knox Co. (TN) (6th Cir., 2002)—Abuse case related to "time-out room" abuse.

F.H. v. Memphis City Schools (6th Cir., 2014)—Parents filed child abuse charges against school.

HH v. Moffett & Chesterfield School Bd. (4th Cir., 2009)—Abuse of special education student by teacher and assistant.

Judith Scruggs, Administratrix of Estate of Daniel Scruggs v. Meriden Bd. of Ed., et al. (U.S. District Court, Connecticut, 23005)—Punitive damages against school for "negligence" regarding a student being a victim of bullying and harassment without school action.

Tereance D. and Wanda D. v. Sch. Dist. Philadelphia (E.D. PA, 2008)—District's failure to provide FAPE for a child for many years. Incompetency revealed in many different services.

IV. DUE PROCESS HEARINGS

J.D.B. v. North Carolina (2011)—A thirteen-year-old girl was interrogated without being given her rights under the Miranda warning. Is a child's age relevant in these cases?

Maroni v. Pemi-Baker Regional School District (1st Cir., 2003)—Ruling that parents can pursue claims relative to IDEA provisions without hiring an attorney.

M.L. v. Federal Way School District (WA) (9th Cir., 2004)—Special education teacher was not included in IEP team. FAPE was violated.

Schaffer v. Weast (546 U.S., 2005)—Burden of proof concerning IEP challenges is upon the party seeking changes in the program.

Zachary Deal v. Hamilton Dept. of Education (TN Due Process Decision, 2001)—Extensive consideration of due process including procedural safeguards and other problems.

V. TEACHER'S RIGHTS

DeYoung v. Commission on Professional Competency (California Court of Appeal, 2nd District, 7-30-14)—Case of teacher competency.

Friedrichs v. California Teachers Association (No. 14-915)—The U.S. Supreme Court is reviewing the *Friedrichs v. California* case regarding the collection of dues from nonmembers of the National Education Association. The teachers have refused to pay such fees on the basis of the First Amendment. Ruling is pending.

LAUSD v. Superior Crt. (Los Angeles)—Teresa Watanabe, "Judges Rule Against Letting Public See LAUSD Teachers' Performance," *Los Angeles Times*, July 23, 2014.

Neily v. Manhattan Beach USD (California Crt. of Appeal, 2nd Dist., Div. 8, January 27, 2011)—Case of teacher status as being probationary or temporary.

Settlegoode v. Portland Public Schools (9th Cir., 2004)—Special education teacher advocates for students and was terminated. First Amendment rights were violated.

Student Success Act of 2011 (Florida) was unanimously upheld by the U.S. Court of Appeals, 11th Dist., Atlanta, July 7, 2015. Fifty percent of a teacher's evaluation is to be based on the results of the Florida Comprehensive Assessment Test (FCAT).

Vergara v. California (Superior Court of the State of California, June 10, 2014)—Case on rights of teachers regarding tenure, seniority, and dismissal questioned.

VI. CURRICULUM STUDIES

Arizona law on Ethnic Studies curriculum, 2010. The 2010 law prohibited an ethnic studies curriculum. A Supreme Court, 9th District, San Francisco, ruled that the facts surrounding the 2010 law suggested that an intent of discrimination was in evidence without question.

VII. STUDENT RIGHTS

C. A. v. William S. Hart Union High School (CA 2nd Dist.), 11-5—Sexual harassment of student.

Dariano v. Morgan Hill Unified School District (767 F.3d 764, 9th Cir., 2014)—Case of students wearing shirts with the American flag in the school.

Frudden v. Pilling (9th Cir. Crt., 2014)—Case on mandatory wearing of school uniform with school motto on it.

Greene v. Camreta (9th Circuit Crt. of Appeals, 2011)—Case of student rights.

Hector v. El Centro Elementary School (California Court of Appeal, Fourth Appellate District, June 24, 2014)—Student bullying and harassment case.

Nathan v. Clovis USD (9th Cir. Crt., 2014)—Student involuntary transfer, 2006.

Sterling v. Borough of Minersville (United States Third Circuit, 99, 1768, 2000)—School personnel should not divulge private information about a student's sexual orientation without authorized permission. Police officers were not entitled to handle private information of the student in this case.

VIII. SCHOOL BOARD RIGHTS

Walnut Valley USD v. Superior Crt. (Rowland USD-1-2-11, California. Court of Appeal, 2nd Dist., Cal., January 27, 2011)—School districts competing for student attendance.

SEARCH AND SEIZURE

Safford v. Redding (557 U.S., 2009)—Were the rights of a student under the Fourteenth Amendment violated when school officials searched her locker when they were told that she had ibuprofen in her locker?

SCHOOL PERSONNEL IMMUNITY

Eason v. Clark County School District (NV) (9th Cir., 2002)—School personnel and legal immunity.

TEACHER IMMUNITY

Fales v. Garst (8th Cir., 2001)—Free speech of teachers and employer's rights.

Appendix B: Selected Significant Legal Events in the History of Education in America

1642 Massachusetts required school inspection and compulsory education

1647 Old Deluder Satan Act required schools in all towns with fifty families

1785 Northwest Ordinance set aside the sixteenth section of government land in each township for school support

1787 Constitutional Convention

Second Northwest Ordinance encouraged schools in the Northwest Territory

1789 U.S. Constitution accepted but left education to the responsibility of the respective states

1791 Bill of Rights ratified with many implications for legal rulings on educational practices

1812 New York created the office of state superintendent of schools

1827 Law requiring high schools passed in Massachusetts

1829 New Jersey general school of law established

1832 Instruction for the blind in Boston and New York

1834 Optional free school law passed in Pennsylvania

1840 Compulsory education act and child labor law in Rhode Island

1849 Principle of general tax for education accepted in New York

1852 Massachusetts compulsory education law passed

1862 Morrill Land-Grant Act passed. Granted thirty thousand acres of land to each state to support at least one college

1866 Fourteenth Amendment protects life, liberty, and property

1869 Fifteenth Amendment guarantees civil rights

1872 Kalamazoo case made taxes legal for high school

1874 Solidified the use of public taxes to support public education; led to rapid growth

1890 Second Morrill Act passed

1914 Smith-Lever Act encouraged agriculture

1917 Smith-Hughes Act encourages vocational schools

1919 Progressive Education Association founded

1925 An Oregon case ruled that private education could not be made illegal by the states

1932 The New Deal programs used federal funds for educational projects

1941 Military training and federal education for defense

1948 The U.S. Supreme Court ruled that religious instruction in public schools was unconstitutional (McCollum case)

1954 *Brown v. Board of Education, Topeka*—The U.S. Supreme Court decision required the integration of public schools and ruled that segregation violated the Fourteenth Amendment

1957 The Soviet Union launched the *Sputnik* satellite, resulting in widespread criticism of American public schools. School reform became a topic of first importance

1958 The National Defense Education Act was passed by the U.S. Congress

1962 Bible reading and prayer ruled unconstitutional in public schools by the U.S. Supreme Court

1964 The Economic Opportunity Act provided for Job Corp and Head Start

The Civil Rights Act was passed

1965 The Elementary and Secondary Education Act provided more federal aid to public schools and called for higher standards of student performance along with school accountability

1967 Age Discrimination Act was passed. No discrimination due to age of the individual

1974 Equal Employment Opportunities Act removed any kind of discrimination for special needs individuals relative to hiring, placement, or remuneration

1975 The Education for All Handicapped Children Act passed into law (P.L. 94-142)

2002 No Child Left Behind Act was passed by Congress. All children were to be brought up to grade by 2014, and all teachers had to become "highly qualified"

2008 Higher Education Opportunities Act set forth information and rules relating to student loans

2010 Race to the Top Program established to boost student academic achievement

2014 Bill to improve access to education for veterans by providing in-state tuition to attend a public university

2015 The Every Child Achieves Act moves away from a testing and punishing system. Ends overuse of testing to assess achievement

2015 Local Control of Education Act extended the Elementary and Secondary Education Act of 1965 to prohibit the federal government from directly or indirectly controlling a state's local specific standards, instructional content, curricula, assessments, or programs of instruction

Glossary of Legal Terms

Academic Freedom: Includes the right of teachers to speak freely about their subject, to experiment with new ideas, and to select appropriate teaching materials and methods without unreasonable interference or restriction from law, institutional regulations, or public pressure.

Administrative Regulation: A precise statement that answers the question of how a policy is to be applied or implemented.

Appeal: A request after a trial by a party that has lost on one or more issues that a higher court review the decision to determine if it was correct.

Appellant: The party who appeals a district court's decision, usually seeking reversal of that decision.

Appellee: The party who opposes an appellant's appeal.

Background Check: A search of a candidate's work history, criminal record, verification of references, and in some cases the candidate's credit record for informational purposes prior to employment.

Bylaws: Procedures by which school boards govern themselves.

Case Law: The law as established in previous court cases. A synonym for *legal precedent*.

Certiorari: A writ seeking judicial review. Orders a lower court to deliver its records in a case so that the higher court may review it.

Civil Law: Infringements of rights—one person to another.

Civil Rights: Rights granted all citizens to be free from discrimination because of race, color, national origin, or sex.

Classified Personnel: Noncertificated personnel that serves the school district.

Common Core Standards: A set of standards for kindergarten through twelfth grade in English language, arts/literacy, and mathematics. Sponsored by the National Governors Association (NGA) and the Council of Chief State School Officers (CCSSO).

Common Law: As distinguished from legislatively created law, the common law consists of those traditionally held legal principles, usually enunciated in court decisions, that derive their force and effect from the historic acceptance and recognition given those principles by a society and its judiciary. Ordinarily, the term refers to the unwritten law of England.

Complaint: A plaintiff's first formal pleading in a civil suit. This document, filed with the court and delivered to the defendant, is intended to inform the defendant of the factual grounds upon which the plaintiff is relying in his lawsuit.

Contract: A promissory agreement between two or more persons that creates, modifies, or destroys a legal transaction.

Contract Mutuality: To understand and agree with the terms of a contract.

Contractual Rights: Teacher rights based on contractual law.

Contributory Negligence: Negligence of the plaintiff combined with the negligence of the defendant.

Corporal Punishment: Punishment that is unreasonable, excessive, and/or cruel is commonly viewed as corporal punishment.

Court: Government entity authorized to resolve legal disputes.

Criminal Law: Violation of criminal codes; misdemeanor or felony.

Damages: A pecuniary compensation or indemnity, which may be recovered in the courts by any person who has suffered loss, detriment, or injury whether to his person, property, or rights through the unlawful act or omission or negligence of another.

de facto: In reality, in act. This term is used to describe an entity or event that is not constituted in a regular and legal fashion but which nonetheless must be accepted for all practical purposes.

Defamation: Scandalous words written or spoken concerning another, tending to the injury of his reputation, for which an action on the case for damages would lie.

Defendant: The party being sued.

de jure: By a lawful title, of right. The contrary of *de facto*.

Detention: A form of punishment used in schools. Usually holding the student from participating in other school activities before, during, or after regular school hours.

Discretionary Power: Involves the exercise of judgment in reaching a decision. Deciding whether to do something.

Dissent: An opinion that disagrees with that of the majority.

Dissention Opinion: An opinion disagreeing with that of the majority.

Employee Right: The ability to engage in conduct that is protected by law or social sanction, free from interference by another party.

Estoppel: Set of doctrines in which a court prevents an action that the litigant normally would have the right to take in order to prevent an unequitable result.

FAPE: Free, appropriate public education for children with disabilities. Granted by the Rehabilitation Act of 1973 and the Individuals with Disability Act of 1975.

Felony: A serious crime. Usually punishable by at least one year in prison.

Hostile Environment: When individuals are harassed by intimidating conditions in the workplace.

Immunity: Refers to the common law concept that school districts are not liable for injuries obtained by others as a result of a civil wrong or injury committed by others employed by it or by someone who works for the district in some capacity.

Indemnity: That which is given a person to prevent his suffering damage. Payment for a loss of some kind such as an injury or any damage that an individual does or could do to another person. Insurance or protection against a loss that occurs or could occur.

In Loco Parentis: In place of parents. Charged with a parent's rights, duties, and responsibilities. In the case of a teacher, this is a condition applying only when the student is under the reasonable control and supervision of the school.

Insubordination: An act by an employee who is asked to do something that is a reasonable or expected responsibility and he or she refuses to do so.

Invitee: An invitee enters an owner's property by way of an expressed or implied invitation of the owner.

Issue: A matter that is in dispute between two or more parties.

Judicial Review: A court's review of a ruling by another governmental body such as a school board in the event of an appeal.

Jury: The group of persons selected to hear the evidence in a trial and render a verdict on matters of fact.

Laches: An unreasonable delay by the plaintiff in bringing the claim.

Law: A rule recognized by the nation or state as binding on its members.

Lawsuit: A legal action started by a plaintiff against a defendant based on a complaint that the defendant failed to perform a legal duty that resulted in harm to the plaintiff.

Libel: Defamation by printed or written communication.

Licensee: A person is a licensee if that person is on the premises only by permission of the owner.

Malfeasance: Misconduct in office.

Malice: Intent to commit an unlawful act without legal justification or excuse or desire to see another person suffer.

Mandamus: A writ, issued from a superior court to an inferior court corporation or officer, which commands the performance of a legally required public act.

Misdemeanor: An offense punishable by one year of imprisonment or less.

Negligence: Lack of care comparable to what would be expected by a competent person in the same situation.

Nolo Contendere: No contest. A plea of nolo contendere has the same effect as a plea of guilty, as far as the criminal sentence is concerned, but it may not be considered as an admission of guilt for any other purpose.

Opinion: A judge's written explanation of the decision of the court.

Ordinance: The term applied to a municipal corporation's legislative enactments. An ordinance should be distinguished from a statute.

Parole Evidence: Prevents the introduction of evidence of prior or contemporaneous negotiations and agreements that contradict, modify, or vary the contractual terms of a written contract.

Plaintiff: The individual that initiates a lawsuit.

Prima Facia: At first view. Presumptions that will prevail if not rebutted or disproved.

Procedural Due Law: In the regular course of administration through courts of justice, according

Procedure: The rules for conducting a lawsuit; there are rules of civil procedure, evidence, bankruptcy, and appellate procedure.

Process: Those rules and forms that have been established for the protection of private rights.

Prose: Representing oneself. Serving as one's own lawyer.

Quantum meruit: What one has earned. Reasonable value of services.

Quid Pro Quo: Harassment that occurs when an employee is asked to provide sexual favors in order to obtain or to remain in employment.

Quo Warranty: A warranty of deed or title.

Quo Warranty Action: Specific form of legal action used to resolve a dispute as to whether a specific person has the legal right to hold the public office that he or she holds.

Reduction in Force: An unrequested leave of absence usually associated with layoffs of personnel due to decreases in student enrollment, budget cuts, or school district reorganization.

Remanded: When a case is sent back to another court or agency for further action.

School Board Policy: Comprehensive statements of decisions, principles, or courses of action that serve toward the achievement of stated educational goals. Policies answer the question of what it is that the school program is to accomplish.

Sexual Harassment: Unwelcomed sexual advances, requests, or demands for sexual favors and other verbal or physical contact of a sexual nature that explicitly or implicitly are suggested as a term or condition of an individual's employment.

Slander: Defamation of spoken word.

Standard of Proof: Degree of proof required. In criminal cases, prosecutors must prove a defendant's guilt "beyond a shadow of a doubt." Other cases require a preponderance of the evidence, and others require clear and convincing proof.

Statute: Law enacted by the legislative power of a country or state.

Statutory Rights: Teacher rights protected by specific laws enacted by government.

Strike: An action that results in stoppage of work and services rendered by the employment group.

Student Detention: Detaining a student during periods when the student would otherwise be free, such as recess, noon, and before and after school.

Student Expulsion: The act of depriving a student the right of membership in the school for some violation or offense that renders him or her unworthy of remaining a member of the school.

Student Suspension: The exclusion of a student from school for a brief but definite period of time.

Substantive Due Process: Guarantees that a person's life, freedom, or property cannot be taken without appropriate governmental justification. Not only guarantees basic procedural rights but also protects basic rights of life, liberty, and property as well.

Tenure: The protection given teachers against arbitrary actions by school officials in the dismissal process. Teachers can be dismissed only for those reasons set forth in law.

Tort: Legal obligation of one party to a victim as a result of civil wrong or injury.

Ultra Vires: A contract made without the authority to do so. The action taken by the body is "beyond the power" given them by laws or corporate charters.

Unrequested Leave of Absence: Commonly due to employee layoffs due to decreased student enrollment, budget cuts, or school district reorganization. Right of recall commonly by seniority.

Verdict: The decision of the judge or trial jury that determines the guilt or innocence of a criminal defendant or determines the outcome of a civil case.

Void: Null, ineffectual, negatory, having no legal force or binding effect. Unable in law to support the purpose for which it was intended.

Warrant: Court authorization to conduct a search or make an arrest.

About the Author

Dr. M. Scott Norton, a former public school mathematics teacher, coordinator of curriculum, and assistant superintendent and superintendent of schools, served as professor and vice-chair of the department of Educational Administration and Supervision at the University of Nebraska, Lincoln, later becoming professor and chair of the department of Educational Administration and Policy Studies at Arizona State University, where he is currently professor emeritus. His primary graduate teaching areas include classes in human resources administration, school superintendency, school principalship, educational leadership, curriculum/instruction, the assistant school principal, and competency-based administration.

Dr. Norton is the author of college textbooks in the areas of human resources administration, the school superintendency, and competency-based leadership, and he has coauthored other books on the school principal as a student advocate, the school principal as a learning leader, and administrative management. He has published widely in national journals in such areas as teacher retention, teacher load, retention of quality school principals, organizational climate, classified personnel in schools, employee assistance programs, distance education, gifted student programs, and others. Three other books authored by Dr. Norton and published by Rowman & Littlefield include: *The Principal as a Learning-Leader: Motivating Students by Emphasizing Achievement*, *Competency-Based Leadership: A Guide for High Performance in the Role of the School Principal*, and *Teachers with the Magic: Great Teachers Change Students' Lives.* He also coauthored with Larry K. Kelly the book *Resource Allocation: Managing Money and People*. He also authored the books *The School Principal as a Human Resources Leader* and *The Assistant Principal's Guide: New Strategies for New Responsibilities*, both published in 2015.

He has received several state and national awards honoring his services and contributions to the field of educational administration from such organization as the American Association of School Administrators, the University Council for Educational Administration, the Arizona Administrators Association, the Arizona Educational Research Association, Arizona State University College of Education Dean's Award for excellence in service to the field, President of the ASU College of Education Faculty Association, and the distinguished service award from the Arizona Information Service.

Dr. Norton's state and national leadership positions have included service as executive director of the Nebraska Association of School Administrators, a member of the Board of Directors for the Nebraska Congress of Parents and Teachers, president of the Nebraska Council of Teachers of Mathematics, president of the Arizona School Administrators Higher Education Division, member of the Arizona School Administrators Board of Directors, staff associate of the University Council for School Administrators, Nebraska State Representative for the National Association of Secondary School Principals, and a member of the Board of Editors for the American Association of School Public Relations.